CINCINNATI
CURIOSITIES

CINCINNATI CURIOSITIES

HEALING POWERS OF THE WAMSLEY MADSTONE, NOCTURNAL EXPLOITS OF OLD MAN DEAD, MAZEPPA'S NAKED RIDE & MORE

To April, a good friend & a wonderful curiosity!

[signature]

GREG HAND

THE
History
PRESS

Published by The History Press
Charleston, SC
www.historypress.com

Front cover: Bartender and moonrise on the Ohio, *Library of Congress*; Mazeppa, sheet music, 1865; Sea serpent, *Illustrated Police News*, 1886.
Back cover: Hog butchers and cabin with ghostly ascension, *Library of Congress*.

First published 2022

Manufactured in the United States

ISBN 9781467152822

Library of Congress Control Number: 2022943527

To Kevin Grace, co-author, colleague, mentor and boon companion

CONTENTS

ACKNOWLEDGEMENTS

S o many people contributed to the content of this volume through questions, suggestions and off-the-wall rumors it taxes my neurons to account for every inspiration. If you have slipped my memory, my apologies. My gratitude overflows to Terry Bailey, Kathi Bastin, Michael Barrett, Ed Beckman, Chaunston Brown, Amy Brownlee, Rick Conner, Richard Arnold Davis, Jerome J. Duwel, Ashley Evans, John Faherty, Otis Flinchpaugh, John Fox, Dave Frondorf, Henry Frondorf, Carol Gibbs, Clyde Gray, Michael Griffith, Kristina Hallez, Steve Hampton, Alan Hand, Joe Hoffecker, Amy Hunter, Abie Ingber, Greg and Liz Kissel, Allie Martin, Kent Meloy, Chris Messick, Michael Monks, Gina Ruffin Moore, Mona Morrow, Kent Mulcahy, Kevin Necessary, Buck Niehoff, Craig Niemi, Hilary Parrish, Mike Perrino, the Reddit mods at r/cincinnati, Dean Regas, Brandon Reynolds, John Rodrigue, Cedric Rose, Paul Ruffing, Liz Scarpelli, Ann Senefeld, Bill Smith, RJ Smith, Anne Delano Steinert, Shawntee Stallworth, David Stradling, Jeff Suess, Nick Swartsell, Jim Tarbell, Mark Thomas, Don Heinrich Tolzmann, Helen Tracey-Noren, Stephen Uhlhorn, John Ventre, Molly Wellmann, Joe Wessels, Howard Wilkinson, Bob Willis, Dann Woellert, and, of course, my at-home focus group: Linda, Jacob & Ina, Autumn and Isaac.

INTRODUCTION

You know Cincinnati's reputation, and so does Urban Dictionary: "A pleasantly bland and annoyingly conservative city that's inexpensive to live in, easy to get around in, and filled with neighborhood festivals. Horribly insular—most people have never been outside the I-275 beltway. Known for chili, goetta, and 'please?' Big on Catholic church festivals during the summers."

We deserve this reputation—or, at least, we earned it—because many people worked very diligently to project exactly that image. Cincinnatians today seem to believe that we have always enjoyed the Opening Day Parade, Skyline chili and Graeter's ice cream. We think it is traditional to celebrate our German heritage during Oktoberfest and our Irish citizenry on St. Patrick's Day. We really think our city was built on seven hills. Like most urban reputations, Cincinnati's is incomplete, only partly true and covers a multitude of sins.

It is symptomatic of Cincinnatians to misremember. For example, when Cincinnati was nicknamed "Porkopolis," it was most definitely not a compliment. Cincinnati still rankles at the opprobrium dished by Frances "Fanny" Trollope in her scathing 1832 indictment of our fair city titled "Domestic Manners of the Americans." A great deal of her bile was directed at our pigs.

Way back in 1987, cultural critic Greil Marcus, a mainstay of the early *Rolling Stone* magazine, turned his attention to the so-called Basement Tapes churned out by Bob Dylan and the musicians who would later become known as The Band. Marcus noted the many tunes Dylan covered or altered from an amazingly bizarre 1952 compilation by musicologist and philosopher Harry Smith called *Anthology of American Folk Music*. Marcus believed that these songs, and Dylan's adaptations of them, provided an unparalleled insight into what he called "the old, weird America," a lost world ignored by the folks who compiled the official histories of inevitable progress, happy and patriotic citizens enjoying the fruits of liberty. Smith and Dylan and Marcus delved into the dark soul of forgotten Americans in the hills, hollers and bayous of a nation fumbling through a fog of superstition and lore, a pre-mythological America in which the role later occupied by television was filled with murder ballads and ecstatic chanting. Compared to popular entertainment, these artifacts stand as anthropological investigations of a strange and foreign culture, but one known intimately to our great-grandparents. Marcus called it the "Old, Weird America."

This book is an attempt to retrieve what's left of that peculiar environment as it can be found amid the detritus of Cincinnati's history. Consider it a journey into the "Old, Weird Cincinnati."

When we talk about Cincinnati's history, for example, we rarely talk about celebratory crowds gathering to watch public floggings, wholesale desecration of downtown Indian mounds, journeys into a hollow earth, high-society membership in occult societies, atheist Sunday schools, UFOs, competitive gluttony, suicide by household product, occasionally nonfatal folk medicine, on-stage nudity, sea monsters, the Ku Klux Klan and rectified whiskey. So, let's turn over some rocks and see what crawls out, shall we?

If you are going to follow me into the past, you must leave some stuff behind. We're not going very far, just 100 or 150 years back, but you will generally have to get by without airplanes, automobiles, television, motion pictures, radio, computers, cellphones, air conditioning, credit cards, zippers, refrigeration, plastics, crosswalks, antibiotics and a few other things. It's a different place.

Cincinnati in 1890, to pick one random census, was home to some 300,000 people. It was the ninth-largest city in the United States, and at that time Brooklyn was counted separately from New York City. Cincinnati was also thoroughly corrupt. For most of the period covered by this book—primarily 1870 to 1920—the city was ruled by a political machine run by a man named George Barnsdale Cox, still infamous today by his nickname, "Boss Cox."

You must also leave behind any concept of equality of the sexes. The period covered by this book was a man's world. It was years before women got the vote. There was no such thing as dating as we know it. Remember the old Henny Youngman joke?

Who was that lady I saw you with last night?
That was no lady. That was my wife!

That's the way it worked. If you were seen in public with a woman, it was assumed you were intimately acquainted. If she wasn't your wife, she was your mistress or one of "those" women.

Also, forget about Newport. Naughty Newport didn't take off until the 1920s, when Prohibition opened up opportunities just as Cincinnati was finally cleaning up its act. In the Naughty Nineties, the real action was on the north side of the river.

Almost all of Cincinnati's 300,000 people lived downtown, in Over-the-Rhine and the West End. A few wealthy pioneers edged up the hillsides heading toward Clifton, Walnut Hills and Mount Auburn, but those were still fairly remote and somewhat rural areas. This was an eminently walkable city, and people walked everywhere. Automobiles had not yet usurped the streets, jaywalking did not exist and our streets were crowded with horses, bicycles, peddlers' carts and pedestrians.

Cincinnati craved entertainment and thrived on sensational, tawdry, melodramatic and risqué spectacles, much as we do today.

Anything was fair game for a bet. The sports pages, dominated by boxing, horse racing and the increasingly popular baseball, reflected this. Today, we think of sport as wholesome athletic endeavors infused by the spirit of fair play. In the 1890s, a "sport" was a gambler. It wasn't just Pete Rose. Back then, everybody bet on baseball.

From the moment the first settlers climbed ashore at Yeatman's Cove in 1788, Cincinnati gained a reputation as an outpost of the Wild West. We have forgotten that some of our early citizens were scalped on Main Street by Indigenous people unwilling to give up their hunting grounds. We have forgotten that our ancestors, on long winter nights, told blood-curdling tales about the ancient spirits still haunting the Ohio River Valley and the artifacts unearthed as we built a city here.

Chapter 1

THE OLD WEIRD CINCINNATI

Back in 1841, a couple of years after the town celebrated its fiftieth birthday, Cincinnati's population topped fifty thousand people. The future downtown area between the riverfront and the Miami and Erie Canal (soon to earn its nickname as "The Rhine") was filling fast, and investors looked for cheaper properties in the outlying areas "Over-the-Rhine," up the slopes of Mount Adams and even into the West End on the swampy Millcreek floodplain.

Blocking the way westward was a man-made hillock labeled "Ancient Mound" on the 1838 map of the city. Among the last remnants of an array of prehistoric earthworks found by the first settlers, this mound blocked the intersection of Mound and Fifth Streets. It had to go. Henry A. Ford and Kate B. Ford, in their 1881 *History of Cincinnati*, describe its demolition:

In November, 1841, the large tumulus near the corner of Fifth and Mound streets was removed, in order to extend Mound street across Fifth and grade an alley. A little above the level of the surrounding surface, near the centre of the mound, were found a large part of a human skull and two bones of about seven inches length, pointed at one end. It was undoubtedly the grave of a Mound Builder, probably a great dignitary of his tribe.

Under the fragmentary skull of the buried Builder was a bed of charcoal, ashes and earth, and therein a very remarkable inscribed stone which, after much discussion, including the publication of Mr. Clarke's interesting pamphlet in vindication of its authenticity, has been pronounced a genuine relic of the period of the Mound Builders.

THE CINCINNATI TABLET.

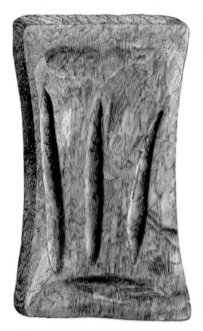

The Cincinnati Tablet continues to inspire debate about its function. *From "Prehistoric Remains," by Robert Clarke, 1878.*

The "remarkable inscribed stone" was immediately christened the Cincinnati Tablet, and no one had any idea what it was. Over the years, theories abounded. Was it a talisman? A calendar? An astronomical observatory? A fabric pattern? A pagan idol? An ancient tattoo "flash"? Maybe the key to saving mankind? You are free to hypothesize because there is still no unanimous agreement about the artifact.

As Ford suggests, the Cincinnati Tablet was initially proclaimed a fake and a fraud. This was a period when American cities took great pride in their antiquities (even while demolishing them for road improvements), so a debate raged for some time until the 1876 publication of *The Pre-Historic Remains Which Were Found on the Site of the City of Cincinnati, Ohio with a Vindication of the "Cincinnati Tablet"* by Robert Clarke, a Cincinnati publisher and bookseller. Clarke traced the provenance of the artifact in such detail that its authenticity was almost universally accepted. The Cincinnati Tablet was donated to the Cincinnati Historical Society, where it resides today among the collections of the Cincinnati Museum Center.

Since the publication of Clarke's book, several similar tablets have been discovered at locations associated with the Adena people who lived in Ohio from about 1000 BC to about 200 BC.

Ford related theories then current (1881) that the tablet might have been a calendar or a stamp for marking fabric or leather with a design. He also noted the resemblance to Egyptian artifacts that were just then catching the public's attention.

In recent years, anthropologist William Romain and other scholars have developed detailed analyses of the geometry of the Adena tablets. Romain suggests that the Cincinnati Tablet was used to locate the rising of the sun and moon at key times of the year. Another interpretation, proposed by amateur archaeologist Frank Otto and others, is incorporated into the Ohio History Connection's online survey of Adena culture:

> *Besides being made of sandstone, the Berlin, Wilmington, Keifer, Cincinnati, and Low tablets are grooved on the back side much like whetstones, which were used for sharpening bone needles. This suggests that the tablets could have been used for tattooing. The engraved surface, covered with paint, could be pressed against a person's body, stamping it with the image. Then the design could be tattooed into the skin using fine bone needles sharpened in the grooves on the back side of the tablet.*

Other interpretations of the Cincinnati Tablet and the other Adena tablets have been all over the intellectual map. One investigator notes that the Cincinnati Tablet has several dots, arranged in groups of eight, six, four and two, and somehow connects this to the diameter of the Sun (864,336 miles). Yet another finds "several fetal designs that have been interpreted as symbolical of those gestative and procreative mysteries that must have powerfully affected the minds of man in the remotest early ages."

Still another theory is that the Cincinnati Tablet "speaks a universal language…the master key of all the mound builders' mysteries, wonderful culture and high intelligence shown and handed down to civilization of the present day for our good and welfare." Speculation has been published that the Cincinnati Tablet and related stones were Masonic talismans or related to the horned serpent idols of Central America or a predictor of global magnetic reversals. And then there is one researcher who concluded, "Scholarship is dumb and imagination is the only interpreter of these strange mementos."

ETIDORHPA AND THE THEOSOPHISTS

The name of the creator of the Cincinnati Tablet is unknown. The creator of *Etidorhpa*—a close runner-up for the strangest Queen City artifact—is not only known but very well known and even memorialized. John Uri Lloyd published this extremely peculiar novel in 1901 to expound upon a number of esoteric beliefs floating through Cincinnati at that time. (The title is the goddess *Aphrodite* spelled backward.) Lloyd, for whom the Lloyd Library on Plum Street is named, claimed that this book was a manuscript dictated to a man named Drury by a mysterious entity named I-Am-the-Man, variously known as The-Man-Who-Did-It. The narrator leads Drury on a journey through a cave in Kentucky into the center of the Earth—which is hollow—and encompasses practical alchemy, secret Masonic orders, hallucinogenic drugs, the Hollow Earth theory and techniques for transcending the physical realm. It gradually dawns on Drury that this journey is as much spiritual as physical. Along the way, I-Am-the-Man expounds on gravity, volcanoes and other phenomena.

J. Augustus Knapp's illustrations to John Uri Lloyd's *Etidorhpa* strongly suggest the use of psychedelic substances. *From* Etidorhpa *by John Uri Lloyd, 1896.*

Lloyd was a true Cincinnati eccentric. He was a proponent of eclectic medicine at a time when Cincinnati was a hotbed of medical innovation and dispute. At one time, the city supported nine medical colleges, each promoting a particular brand of medicine. The eclectics were into botanical preparations, including a popular cannabis extract. Lloyd and his brothers made a fortune creating eclectic pharmaceutical concoctions. Prosperity gave John Uri Lloyd the time to dive into the philosophical rabbit hole that yielded *Etidorhpa*.

As if Lloyd's book wasn't bizarre enough, it was illustrated by a truly curious chap named J. Augustus Knapp, who led the Cincinnati Chapter of the Theosophists, an esoteric religious movement, devoted to explorations of the occult arts. While Knapp headed the local cabal, Cincinnati Theosophists were so active that the national conference of this arcane order convened here in 1899.

Knapp, a native of Newport, Kentucky, was a contemporary of Cincinnati artists Frank Duvenek and Henry Farny. Knapp studied at the McMicken School of Design, which later became the Cincinnati Art Academy. He found work as a designer and lithographer with many Cincinnati printing companies. While at Standard Publishing, Knapp met Curtis Gates Lloyd, the youngest brother of John Uri Lloyd. Through this association, Knapp collaborated frequently with the Lloyds on various projects.

While they were working on *Etidorhpa*, Knapp and John Uri Lloyd lived within walking distance of each other in Norwood. After World War I, Knapp moved to Los Angeles, California, where he got involved in the very early days of the movie industry.

A MONUMENT TO A HOLLOW EARTH

Lloyd's incorporation of Hollow Earth theory into his magnum opus draws on a truly whacko concept with a sterling Cincinnati pedigree.

Have you ever wondered why Santa Claus lives at the North Pole, of all places? The answer might reside in a small urban park that was once a graveyard in Hamilton, Ohio. You will find there the Hollow Earth Monument, perhaps the most unusual tombstone ever raised in the United States. It is certainly among the very few memorials erected to celebrate an amazingly crackpot geographical theory.

Hamilton's Hollow Earth Monument marks the gravesite of Captain John Cleves Symmes. He believed that the earth was hollow and that we could

The Symmes family spent decades trying to mount an expedition to prove that the Earth is hollow, its interior habitable and easily accessible from the polar regions. *From* The Symmes Theory of Concentric Spheres *by Americus Symmes, 1878.*

gain entrance to the interior of our planet through huge holes that pierced the North and South Poles. Symmes believed the climate at the poles was balmy and temperate, once travelers got beyond a protective ring of ice and snow—an ideal hiding place for Santa Claus.

If Symmes's name sounds familiar, it's because he is the nephew and namesake of the same John Cleves Symmes who helped create Cincinnati. The younger Symmes earned fame as a hero during the War of 1812 and spent the rest of his life, and his reputation, propounding his crackpot theory.

Symmes developed his Hollow Earth theory while living in Newport, Kentucky, and sent pamphlets to every potential donor in the United States and Europe. He hoped to gather enough money to mount an expedition to the North Pole. United States president John Quincy Adams was reportedly on the verge of awarding federal funding to the Symmes expedition when he was voted out of office. Symmes died with his vision unfulfilled.

Symmes's son, Americus Vespucci Symmes, took up the torch and published a book to popularize his late father's Hollow Earth ideas. Americus claimed an 1871 expedition led by Cincinnatian Charles Francis Hall had verified his father's theories, even though that voyage turned around far short of the North Pole. John Uri Lloyd was inspired to write his fantasy novel *Etidorhpa* in part on the Hollow Earth theory. Symmes's theory also inspired Jules Verne to compose his novel *A Journey to the Center of the Earth*.

Alas, Americus, too, died before anyone traveled far enough north, or south, to prove or disprove John Cleves Symmes's theory. Americus erected the Hollow Earth Monument over his father's grave in 1840, and it has attracted curious visitors ever since.

WITCHES AND NECROMANCERS

The arcane philosophies that birthed the Hollow Earth theory and *Etidorhpa* were far more sophisticated than the beliefs of most Cincinnatians, who firmly believed in the power of witchcraft.

To give one example, the Schefflers, an entire family of German immigrants, marched into the Bremen Street police station in Over-the-Rhine one night in 1883 and begged for sanctuary to escape a haunted house. Their home on Liberty Street, they said, had been bewitched by a neighbor named Frau Landecker, who had cast spells on them through homemade potions. It appears the family had procured a variety of medicinal teas from Frau Landecker but had, according to the *Cincinnati Gazette* of March 27, 1883, experienced untold mischief:

> *Peculiar noises were heard about the house. Members of the family were unceremoniously jerked from their beds. Black and shadowy figures were seen as they glided past, and not only seen, but felt as they took malicious enjoyment in pulling hair, pinching noses, jerking dresses, and such ghostlike pranks ad infinitum.*

In 1869, a widow named Amanda Truman claimed witchcraft by spiritualists as the cause of several deaths in the Sedamsville area. According to the *Cincinnati Commercial* of June 4, 1869, Truman asserted that she had proof:

Let any person draw the picture of the spiritualist, take a gun, load it with silver and shoot at the picture, and see if the devil won't defend them. There are a great many people that die suddenly of inflammation of the brain, stomach and bowels, which is caused by these wretches throwing wind into them.

In 1875, a feud between two Italian families on Front Street led to charges of witchcraft. The father of one family shot the cat belonging to an old woman living nearby. She supposedly cursed the newborn child of the cat-killer's family, and it wasted away for several months until the family called in Alexander Schilling, Cincinnati's resident exorcist at the time. According to the Cincinnati Enquirer of September 12, 1875:

It will be remembered that it was this professor of devil-driving who not long ago rescued a child from an evil-working old woman on Cross street. Dr. Twelve-and-a-Half-Cents no sooner saw the child, or rather the shape of the child, than he pronounced it a victim of witchcraft. The parents "knew it" as soon as he said so.

Schilling concocted a potion to be rubbed on the sickly child and ordered the child's mattress to be cut open.

Just as was expected, they found within the unquestionable tracks of a witch. Among the feathers was something like the comb of a chicken, beautifully ruffled and frilled, and composed of many colored feathers. Besides this chicken's chignon, there was also found an equally wonderfully formed wreath, not yet quite full grown.

Although the exorcist ordered these things burned, the sickly child died anyway.

Witchcraft and necromancy destroyed the marriage of William H. Lauterback in 1922. Was he really a harmless old Sedamsville gardener or a dangerous necromancer? Some sort of dark wizard? Or was he just a simple German immigrant who eked out a humble existence, toiling among his plants?

Lauterback was sixty-five and a widower twice over when he married his third wife. According to their marriage license, Katherine Darby was forty-four, but she claimed she was really thirty-nine. It was the third marriage for each of them, and it lasted less than four months.

A grey demon who squawked like a parrot and a somber skeleton figured into the 1922 divorce of Katherine and William Lauterback. *From* Cincinnati Post, *April 18, 1922.*

Lauterback testified that Katherine complained about his muddy shoes when he worked in his garden, told him that he was too old and dirty for her and threw all his clothing out of his own house. She had him arrested when he tried to clean up the mess, so he filed for divorce. Katherine countersued. And that's when this became one of the more interesting divorce cases in Cincinnati history.

Lauterback, his wife asserted, stayed awake until all hours reading books about the spirit world. His reading habits would be neither here nor there, Katherine testified, but her husband's occult pursuits had unleashed hostile entities that tormented her constantly. She claimed he practiced summoning these evil beings all night by lamplight. As the *Cincinnati Post* of April 18, 1922, reported:

> *One, she claims, was a devilish creature with horns, who wore grey tights. This "devil," according to Mrs. Lauterback, sometimes accompanied by similar creatures, would jump about her while she lay in bed and while she worked in her rooms. He "pecked" and "poked" at her and uttered parrot-like cries, said Mrs. Lauterback.*

As if having a grey demon and its minions hopping and squawking around the house wasn't enough, Katherine told the court that there was another eerie visitor as well: "The other, she said, was a regular skeleton, somber and gruesome, which would walk up to her or stoop over her as she lay in bed, without touching her, and stare into her face, without uttering a sound."

She also claimed that Lauterback had some supernatural power over her because she never wanted to marry the old guy to begin with, but he had beguiled her, she said, through the power of a medallion he always wore around his neck.

For his part, Lauterback seemed completely confused by the whole matrimonial disaster. Both of Lauterback's previous wives were now dead—the first at a young age after bearing four children, the second in 1920 after raising the first wife's children to adulthood. Lauterback told the court he would never marry again.

Katherine told the court that Lauterback once told her he thought she had more money than he discovered after they were married. He filed for divorce when he learned she was poor, she said. Lauterback insisted his nighttime reading had nothing to do with spirits. It was all about astronomy and the motion of stars and planets. (As a gardener, it is likely Lauterback was reading an almanac.)

The grey devil and the gruesome skeleton apparently never showed up in court. The judge ruled in Lauterback's favor on grounds of cruelty, granting him a clean break without alimony. Lauterback died three years later and is buried at Spring Grove Cemetery next to his second wife. The house supposedly infested by the supernatural antagonists still stands at 655 Delhi Road in Sedamsville.

CURED BY A MADSTONE

Cincinnati sincerely believed in magical cures for certain diseases. For more than fifty years, when mad dogs bit, victims from across Ohio, Indiana and Kentucky rushed to a farm outside Cleves, Ohio, to avoid horrific death from rabies by applying the Wamsley madstone.

Few today have even heard of madstones, but well into the 1900s, madstones were treasured amulets promising relief from rabies and snakebite, as well as other ailments. Sometimes called bezoar stones, madstones commonly came from the stomachs of ungulate animals, particularly deer and most particularly albino deer. It is obvious that some madstones had different origins because they are described as found along roadsides or in mineral deposits. All shared a reputation for drawing poisons out of the body.

The Wamsley madstone was owned by Moses B. Wamsley, who lived on a big farm along River Road near Cleves. Wamsley claimed to have acquired the stone in 1844, when he was about thirty years old, from a family named Tanner in Burlington, Kentucky. One of Wamsley's cattle was bitten by a rabid dog and blew foam into Wamsley's eye. He was advised to find the Tanners to be cured by their madstone.

Impressed by the results, Wamsley offered to buy the stone for twenty-five dollars, but the Tanners refused to sell. The Tanners had brought the stone, described as walnut-sized, to Kentucky from their ancestral home in Virginia. At length, they offered to sell a chip from their stone to Wamsley and brought in a file, which had no effect on the stone. With a hammer and chisel, the Tanners broke their madstone into three pieces, one of which passed to Wamsley for twenty-five dollars.

The Wamsley stone is described as flinty, about the size of the end of a man's thumb, perfectly transparent and resembling "California diamond"—a glassy variety of opal also known as hyalite.

Madstones supposedly worked not only as a cure but as a diagnostic test as well. The stone was placed on the patient near a wound. If the stone adhered to the patient's skin, it was left attached as long as necessary. When the stone fell off, it was washed in warm milk and reapplied until it would no longer adhere. If the stone never adhered, the patient was assumed to have no poison in his system. Madstones are primarily described as a treatment for rabies but were also used in cases of snakebite and some chronic illnesses.

When Moses Wamsley died in 1898, he bequeathed the madstone to his younger daughters, Fannie and Belle. The first mention of the Wamsley madstone was in the *Cincinnati Gazette* in 1869, and it is apparent that the stone had been effecting cures for some years prior to that date. The Wamsley stone made the news into the 1900s, when it was employed to cure a patient from Van Wert, Ohio.

The Wamsley stone was among a very few madstones reported in this general region. In addition to the Tanner madstone in Burlington, there was a famous madstone in Greencastle, Indiana, and one stored at the Ohio Statehouse. As late as 1911, a madstone was found in an albino deer killed on the Texas ranch owned by Cincinnatian Charles Taft (brother of President and Chief Justice William Howard Taft). In 1905, the *Cincinnati Post* described a large madstone stored by Cincinnati realtor Albert Williamson in a vault at the Northside Bank.

Beginning as early as the 1870s, newspapers reported that patients endured the antibiotic "Pasteur Treatment" for rabies rather than relying on madstones. After 1910 or so, science won out, and madstones were no longer mentioned except as curiosities.

A medical journal from 1890 described the Wamsley madstone and cautioned doctors and scientists from too much skepticism:

> *Unless she is too ill to do so, old Mrs. Wamsley always applies it. Her faith in its curative powers, is only equaled by her trust in divine revelation. She has performed hundreds of cures with it, unless these seeming cures were coincidences, and we doctors had better not spring any tremendous discussion on the subject.*

DIAGNOSES FROM BUMPY HEADS

Today, we think of phrenology as a classic pseudoscience, concerned with reading personality through the contours of the head, but Cincinnatians truly believed in the powers of phrenology to diagnose diseases and personality disorders.

For most of two decades in the 1880s and 1890s, Cincinnati's leading phrenologist cultivated something of a national reputation. Among the heads whose bumps he analyzed were Sarah Bernhardt, Mark Twain, Lillie Langtry, Henry Ward Beecher and other celebrities of the era.

Edgar C. Beall was a true believer and had his own definition of phrenology, which he outlined in an advertisement in the *Cincinnati Post* of July 30, 1886:

> *Phrenology means mental science, and includes all systematized knowledge pertaining to character and intelligence. As an art, it enables us to read the mind by the diameter of the head, or the distance upward, forward and backward from the ear, taking into account the temperament, quality of the organization, &c., &c. It is not, as many suppose, a science of cranial "hills and hollows," but a subject of infinite dignity and practical value.*

Born just outside Cincinnati in Lockland, Beall invested years in the study of phrenology, but he was a lifelong seeker of essential truths in many fields. He achieved certification from the American Institute of Phrenology in New York and then moved back to the Cincinnati area and enrolled at the Medical College of Ohio, while simultaneously studying theology on the side. His investigations resulted in an explosively controversial critique of religion. The *Cincinnati Enquirer* predicted a stormy reception:

> *Edgar C. Beall, the well-known phrenologist of this city, has written a book called "The Brain and the Bible," which is the latest addition to the infidel literature of the day and at the same time is an exposition of the principles and philosophy of phrenology applied to religion. The book is written in good, terse, clear English, and will, doubtless, be the cause of much comment and controversy.*

Beall summarizes his controversial "infidel" thesis in the book's final chapter:

> *In opposing Christianity, therefore, as a religious system, we denounce simply its pernicious doctrines and absurd dogmas which are contradicted by science and plainly inimical to the highest happiness of mankind. Among these are chiefly the existence of a personal God and a personal Devil, the fall of man, the scheme of salvation by faith, and endless torment to those who reject Christ as a divine savior.*

Despite his controversial writings and association with known agnostics, Beall remained popular in Cincinnati. He regularly lectured on phrenology to packed auditoriums, and the newspapers hired him to provide character studies of people in the news, locally and nationally.

These newspaper analyses indicate the fundamental weakness of phrenology—it is a classic example of the fallacy known as "post hoc, ergo propter hoc." In other words, because some factor existed before a particular result, that factor must be the cause of the result. Beall knew quite a bit about the people he analyzed—Admiral George Dewey, George B. "Boss" Cox, Rabbi Isaac M. Wise—and so his "phrenographs" essentially reinforced popular opinion of these individuals.

In addition to phrenology, Beall was a lifelong advocate of hygiene. Today, we think of hygiene as basic cleanliness. Back in the day, hygiene covered a lot of behaviors, including diet, exercise, clothing and even mental, moral and sexual habits.

This interest in hygiene led Beall to write another controversial book. For once, Cincinnati's prudery had nothing to do with it. By 1900, Beall had moved to New York City to assume editorship of the *Phrenological Journal*, official publication of the Phrenological Institute. In 1905, he published a

A Character Study of George Barnsdale Cox.
(From a Personal Examination by Edgar C. Beall, M. D.)

A Cincinnati phrenologist delved into the psyche of George "Boss" Cox, showing Cincinnati's political tyrant had weak ideality but strong sex love. *From* Cincinnati Post, *May 19, 1897.*

volume titled *The Life Sexual: A Study of the Philosophy, Physiology, Science, Art, and Hygiene of Love.* In other words, Beall published a sex manual, although it was a sex manual of its time, with lots of advice about good habits and very few revelations about the actual mechanics involved. Still, it was salacious enough to get banned by the post office. Theodore Schroeder, in a 1911 book supporting freedom of the press, specifically highlights the censorship of Beall's book as an ill-considered act:

I have read much of this book and can not for the life of me conceive why it should be deemed offensive, because the book is written in a refined style and is instructive. The opening chapter is devoted to a strong criticism of "The Ban upon Sexual Science," and maybe therein lies the cause of complaint.

Interestingly, Beall never married, although his *Life Sexual* book was emphatic in support of marriage. Perhaps it was to offer some researcher an opportunity to solve this conundrum that Beall made his final and greatest contribution to phrenology: his own brain. A few years before he died, Beall telephoned the medical school of Cornell University and informed the doctors there that he had willed his body to be dissected and studied for scientific research. "When you get it," he told the faculty, "pay particular attention to a study of my brain."

The body arrived at Cornell's medical campus in New York City after Beall's death in 1930. According to the newspapers, "His is said to have been a very abnormal brain."

SUNDAY SCHOOL FOR ATHEISTS

If Theosophy, witchcraft, phrenology and folk medicine were too esoteric for you, Cincinnati was also home to a thriving agnostic community, founded by a lawyer named Charles Sparks. Agnosticism was as close to actual atheism as you could get in Cincinnati, but there were enough atheists in our city to form an entire congregation with regular services and their own Sunday school. It seems contradictory: a Sunday school for nonbelievers. But, with the support of a prominent attorney, Cincinnati created just such an institution.

The front page of the *Cincinnati Post* for January 22, 1901, contained a relatively small item, below the fold, that really riled up Cincinnati. The headline read, simply, "Agnostic Sunday School."

An Agnostic Sunday School will be opened in Cincinnati the first Sunday in February. Attorney Chas. S. Sparks will be the superintendent, and Oscar J. Hazel Secretary. Twelve children, ranging from 7 to 14 years, have, through their parents, promised to attend. Mrs. Ruth Hazel, of Ninth and Walnut, has volunteered to teach, and others will be appointed as the school increases.

The news landed like a bomb in the Queen City. The *Post* reported a few days later that only two topics dominated the sermons being written by Cincinnati ministers that week: agnosticism and the death of Queen Victoria. Consequently, most Cincinnatians heard sermons either condemning the agnostic "church" or praising Christian womanhood that week. The Reverend Charles M. Fillmore of Carthage Christian Church typified the lot with his proposed sermon on "The Sin of Unbelief."

It is true that Attorney Sparks and his "congregation" preached that God did not exist. He was a follower of Robert G. Ingersoll, the "Great Agnostic," who spent the final decades of the 1800s writing and lecturing on the evils of organized religion. Sparks laid out a basic humanist agenda for his Agnostic Sunday School:

The children will be taught virtue, honesty, self-esteem, love of country, love of home and kindred, and the brotherhood of mankind. To do good for sake of good and the joy it brings. They will be taught according to Sparks' belief that it is an insult to pray to God, but that children should be made to remember that their food is provided by their parents. They will be taught to be good every day in the week; to so conduct themselves that they may enjoy slumber without troubled thoughts; to be kind and generous, and mindful of the feelings, and sentiments of others, and to avoid evil associates. The precepts will be laid down that noble actions bring their own rewards.

The *Cincinnati Post* drafted one of its copy boys to attend Agnostic Sunday School and printed a report on February 12, 1901:

I counted 20 children in the Sunday School. First we sang, and then the men told ghost and spirit stories which were very frightful. Some of them said God never existed on this earth, and that no person could explain what the soul was and what it was made of or how it made its flight from the body to heaven.

While Cincinnati ministers fulminated, the creation of the Agnostic Sunday School made national news. The *Literary Digest* of June 8, 1901, blamed the entire Midwest for this outrageous apostasy: "Recent newspaper reports from Cincinnati indicate that the great Middle West still continues to be fertile in new religious movements. The latest 'sect' is composed of agnostics, and is said to be based on the teachings of the late Robert G. Ingersoll."

Cincinnati, and the national media, really went ballistic when Sparks announced that he was introducing an agnostic marriage ceremony through a June ceremony. Sparks's marriage vows were innovative on a number of points. The husband promised to make his wife happy, to avoid drunkenness, to buy a life insurance policy naming his wife as beneficiary and to not oppose a request for divorce. The wife promised not to bear children unless she believed that she and her husband were happy and compatible, to divorce him if not and to educate any children and raise them as agnostics. Most upsetting to many Cincinnatians, the wife did not promise to obey her husband.

The agnostic marriage vows were unveiled on June 2, 1901, at the Mercantile Library Building when Fred Federle, lapsed Catholic, and Martha Seamans, erstwhile Baptist, were joined in matrimony by Justice of the Peace Alex Roebling after Sparks administered the vows. According to the *Post* of June 3, 1901, "The name of God was nowhere mentioned....The bride did not promise to 'obey.'"

The wedding made national news, reaching the pages of the *New York Times*. There was even more nationwide publicity when Sparks announced an agnostic funeral service. The Cincinnati agnostics remained a small group despite offering free beer at their summer picnics. By the end of the year, Sparks's agnostic "sect" had forty to fifty adult adherents, while between thirty-five and forty children attended Sunday school. The *Post* of May 21, 1901, reflected the feelings of Cincinnati in an editorial:

> *It is the right of every man to believe or not to believe. It is the right of Mr. Sparks, but when he attempts to make Agnostics of tender children by ridicule, the hollowness of which they cannot comprehend, there is a protest. Common decency and respect for the wishes of good men and women should force Mr. Sparks to halt.*

Halt he did not, but the movement eventually lost steam. Sparks announced plans to debate various preachers and to build an agnostic temple in Cincinnati. Neither occurred, and it appears the congregation dissolved after a few years.

Sparks continued to practice law and occasionally provided commentary about agnosticism for the newspapers. He succumbed to stomach cancer in 1929 and is buried in Clermont County with his wife and some of his children.

THE LOCKLAND UFO

While the agnostics denied the existence of a higher power, some Millcreek Valley commuters believed what they saw with their own eyes.

At 6:00 a.m. on Friday, December 2, 1898, six men, all residents of Lockland, stood on a street corner waiting for the streetcar to carry them to their jobs downtown. As the men chatted, exchanging the usual pleasantries, according to the *Cincinnati Enquirer* of December 3, 1898, one man gasped in amazement and pointed upward:

> *To the great astonishment of the observers they perceived in the dim, misty light, a curious object that was traveling at a high rate of speed in a southeasterly direction. The mysterious thing was egg-shaped, although its exact lines were partially obscured by the mist. It emerged from the gloom in the north. The object was enveloped in a faint light. At an even distance on each side of it two small but dazzling lights kept the main object company.*

This was almost exactly five years before the Wright brothers took off from Kitty Hawk.

OHIO RIVER SEA MONSTERS

It wasn't only aerial manifestations that inspired amazement in old Cincinnati.

In the dim, predawn light of Friday, January 11, 1878, Ben Karrick was driving his horse-drawn delivery wagon over the Roebling Suspension Bridge when he saw a most unusual sight in the Ohio River below: a sea serpent. He told the *Cincinnati Gazette*, "Protruding from the water some twelve or fifteen feet was what seemed to be the head of a huge serpent or animal, that was rushing through the water at a very rapid rate, and occasionally lashing the water with its tail into a perfect foam."

Karrick told the newspaper that the beast made a noise similar to the deep lowing of a cow, interspersed with a loud hissing noise. It looked, he said, nothing at all like a cow: "Its head and neck seemed to me to be covered by a black glossy substance like hair, and further back from the head, the hide looked like that of an alligator. The head was shaped somewhat similar to that of a sea horse, which we have so often seen in pictures."

The late 1870s were rife with sightings of sea monsters in the Ohio River. *From the* Illustrated Police News, *August 7, 1886.*

The great serpent swam rapidly upstream, Karrick said, and headed toward the Ohio shore before it disappeared from sight.

A few days later, the *Gazette* carried a letter on the front page suggesting that Karrick's monster was none other than the great serpent of Clermont County's Hartman Mill dam that had escaped some years prior. That serpent was reputedly fifteen to twenty feet long and as thick as the body of a man and lived in the pool of a dammed creek upstream from the Little Miami River. A letter to the *Cincinnati Commercial* recorded memories of the "Great Snake Hunt" of 1847, organized out of Williamsburg, in which a posse armed with "guns, pitch forks, corn knives, clubs and almost every other conceivable weapon" was organized by a couple of local military veterans in a fruitless search for the Hartman Mill monster.

Mr. Karrick's sea serpent matches closely the report, just one day earlier, of a sea serpent swimming farther downstream in the Ohio River. John Davidson, master of the *Silver Moon* steamboat, was docked at Vevay, Indiana, when he saw an amazing apparition. As he wrote to the *Cincinnati Enquirer* of January 11, 1878]:

> *I had no faith in the reports I had read of the river monster, so graphically described in the newspapers, but I am now convinced of the actual existence*

of the terrible beast. At one time it reared its head high above the surface of the water in the manner of the sea lions of the Zoological Gardens of your city. The long pelican beak, the slimy mane, and the extreme serpentine length of the animal answer exactly to the previous descriptions that have been published.

The monster dove beneath the surface before Captain Davidson could call his first mate to witness the beast. The captain had some serious advice for the city of Cincinnati: "I would suggest the employment of your Gatling gun along the banks of the river for a few days, and it is probable the beast can be destroyed and its body captured."

Giant serpents were not, apparently, limited to the Ohio River and its tributaries. In 1885, the *Cincinnati Gazette* described an immense snake terrorizing the inhabitants of Ripley County, Indiana. The edition of August 23 carried a breathless report describing the experience of Thomas Leppar and his grown son, who collected loads of wood to sell in Pierceville. Near Milan,

Mr. Leppar and his son had loaded their wagon with stovewood, and started to drive through the thick undergrowth and tangled bushes which abound in all woods in this section of the county, when all of a sudden young Leppar, who was driving saw the monster with his head lifted five feet from the ground, his eyes flashing fire and darting his forked tongue from his massive mouth with lightning rapidity. The young man, although, as he describes it, "almost paralyzed," had the presence of mind to turn his team short around, thereby avoiding the stroke of the snake, and no doubt saving his horses from the coil of the monster, which meant death.

The Leppars estimated (which the *Gazette* acknowledged might have been affected by "intense excitement") that the giant snake was twenty-four feet long and two feet in diameter. The Leppars' story was corroborated by one John Lane, who was cutting wood in the same area for charcoal. He rushed over with his axe, "but the serpent was thoroughly aroused, and in its fury tore up the ground and lashed into fragments the bushes for yards around."

Although it does not appear that anyone captured or killed any Ohio River sea serpents or Ripley County anacondas, there are records of a very unusual reptile captured from the river at Cincinnati—alligators. The *Cincinnati Gazette* of October 23, 1879, reported that an alligator some three feet in length was snared on the Covington bank. "Since the capture several others of the same species of animal have been seen between the empty coal barges, near the mouth of Willow Run. This is the first time alligators have ascended the Ohio as far as Cincinnati."

A Cincinnati surgeon, A. Jackson Howe, took possession of the captured alligator "for scientific purposes" and had it displayed at the Cincinnati Society of Natural History at 108 Broadway. "The captive is exceedingly pugnacious and vicious. Small boys should not bathe in the river at present."

KU KLUX KLOTHES

On land, Cincinnati had human monsters—and they sold men's clothing. It will not surprise you that Cincinnati was a hotbed of Ku Klux Klan activity, but a haberdashery? It's true. On a drizzly autumn day in 1925, more than two thousand members of the Ku Klux Klan marched through downtown Cincinnati. The procession celebrated the fifth anniversary of the Klan in Cincinnati.

Robed and hooded, but with faces unmasked, the parade was led by Cincinnati's police chief, William Copelan, accompanied by a police escort made up of Copelan's senior staff. Approximately half of the marchers represented Hamilton County Klans, notably the Price Hill contingent, who were first in line among the local organizations. Major national officers were also present, among them Ohio grand dragon Clyde W. Osborne of Youngstown and

Advertising "One Price—One Profit," the Ku Klux Klothes store provided men's fashions in downtown Cincinnati during the 1920s. *From Cincinnati Enquirer, August 22, 1920.*

Theodore Heck Jr., leader of the Hamilton County Klan. Hiram Wesley Evans of Texas, the national grand wizard of the Knights of the Ku Klux Klan, had planned to attend but bailed at the last minute. Grand Dragon Osborne told the *Cincinnati Post* of October 24, 1925, exactly what the Ku Klux Klan was all about:

> *We do not seek to deprive the Jew or Catholic of the right to hold office. However, we do seek to advance and protect Protestant interests by securing proportional share of public representation. We believe in the supremacy of the white man and woman in America. We are opposed to racial equality and are ever ready to promote the best interest of negroes. However, we will*

not tolerate the intermarrying or interbreeding of whites with the black or yellow races. We feel that today the supremacy of the white man in America is menaced seriously.

Although Price Hill led the local Klan in this particular parade, Cincinnati had Klans in many neighborhoods, including Northside, Linwood, Walnut Hills, St. Bernard, Lockland and Norwood. The Klan openly advertised "Klonklaves" or initiation gatherings at the Hamilton County Fairgrounds in Carthage. Major Klan events, including the raising of fiery crosses, took place at a big field near North Bend and Winton Roads in Finneytown. A 1921 initiation ceremony on Wooster Pike near Terrace Park brought out 1,500 men. The Klan even held an initiation of 460 new members in 1922 at the Cincinnati Zoo.

Although the 1925 Klan parade openly advertised the participation of the police chief, no other elected officials participated. No local politicians openly supported or promoted the Klan, although it was rumored that some lent private support. A few authorities publicly opposed the Klan, notably Mayor Louis Nolte of Norwood, whose position did not interfere with his winning two more terms. Nolte announced that the Klan was prohibited from meeting in his city, mostly because they had publicly announced they were going to fill the ranks of the police and fire departments with Klansmen. Nolte told the *Cincinnati Post* of December 2, 1922, "I am opposed to discriminating against any man on account of race or religion. I am a Mason, I belong to the Presbyterian Church, but because a man does not think as I do is no reason for barring him from working for me."

Another vocal opponent of the Klan was Gilbert Bettman Sr., who later became a justice of the Ohio Supreme Court. As state commander of the American Legion, Bettman announced that Klan membership violated the ideals of the American Legion. He told the *Cincinnati Post*, "I would give the men a choice between the Legion and the Klan after explaining that membership in the Klan was not in keeping with Legion principles. If the men choose the Klan then they should be asked to withdraw from the Legion."

The Klan appear to have been most active in the Cincinnati area around 1922, appearing in daylight at a funeral in Reading and getting newspaper coverage for delivering toys and candy to charitable organizations at Christmas.

Perhaps the weirdest manifestation of Klan activity in Cincinnati was a clothing store at the northeast corner of Fourth and Main Streets in the heart of downtown Cincinnati. For months prior to the store's opening, Cincinnati's newspapers were filled with cryptic advertisements hinting that headquarters for the Ku Klux Klan would occupy the building. Here is a sample from the *Cincinnati Enquirer* of July 1, 1920:

> *Ku Klux Klan, Looking Hither And Moving Onward: A fine part of civilization teaches us to love our neighbor as ourself; yet modern society acknowledges no neighbor. Of the essentials and necessities of life, we are mostly ruined not by what we really want, but by what we think we do. Therefore, never go abroad in search of your wants; if they be real wants they will come home in search of you, for he that buys what he does not want will soon want what he cannot buy. Ku Klux Klan throws out a forbearing friendship that saves you a search. It gives you inward strength for your outward view, and offers the most inexpensive fortification in modern society, to wit: Initiation day is not far off now, as you will notice if you are watching headquarters (a whole building).*

And yet, when that building opened, it did not hold the headquarters of the local Ku Klux Klan (most reports have central Klan headquarters at the corner of Allison and Vine) but a haberdashery named Ku Klux Klothes, with the catchy slogan "One Price—One Profit." That price indicated that the local Ku Klux Klan catered to a somewhat upscale crowd, because the "one price" was $33 for a man's suit. In 2021 dollars, that's equivalent to $465—hardly Armani but hardly Big Lots, either.

Ku Klux Klothes operated out of the Main Street location for just a bit over a year before it was bought out by the R.B. Clothing Company, which maintained its anchor store at the northwest corner of Fifth and Elm and used the former Ku Klux Klothes building as a discount annex.

After the Klan parade through downtown, "several thousand" assembled at the Carthage Fair Grounds for speeches, fireworks and the initiation of new members. Grand Dragon Osborne proclaimed the evils of motion pictures produced, he said, by a small group of Jews. The Klan in Ohio was actively engaged in fighting the Catholic influence on public schools.

Not everyone welcomed the Klan to the Queen City. As the Carthage Klonklave disbanded, Klansmen returned downtown to catch trains out of town. There, a crowd of onlookers bombarded them with, according to the *Cincinnati Enquirer* of October 25, 1925, "a fusillade of debris, including eggs of a distinct vintage, tomatoes that had seen better days, potatoes that were still solid, interspersed with larger missiles that resembled cantaloupes."

There were no injuries, and four young men were arrested on disorderly conduct charges.

CINCINNATI BANS MUSIC

Far less serious than the Klan, a rogue organization aimed to strike a blow at a cornerstone of Cincinnati culture—our music. The Society for the Suppression of Music was sprung upon an unsuspecting Cincinnati in November 1879. The newspapers carried a brief classified item that conveyed the flavor of the new organization:

> *Society for the Suppression of Music: Applications for membership in the above society are coming in rapidly—among the latest are Edward Goepper, Wm. W. Taylor, Bellamy Storer, C.F. La Motte, and Frank A. Lee. The reason these well known (former) devotees of Calliope have joined may be learned from the parties themselves by anyone curious to know. The society is now in a flourishing condition, and numbers among its members some of the best of our citizens. Persons desirous of joining should address without delay Judge Longworth, President, or Jno. S. Woods, Treasurer, who will furnish all information on the subject.*

Judging by the evidence, the Society for the Suppression of Music was a joke created by Cincinnati artist Henry Farny and paper merchant John S. Woods. Completely humorous in intent, the society gathered for regular dinners at which members presented hilariously ostentatious reports (some of which saw print in the local newspapers) and awarded each other facetious honors.

Newspapers as far away as Chicago picked up the gag and recommended that their cities should form satellite chapters. The tone (if I may be forgiven a musical metaphor) of the society is reflected in

Music-loving Cincinnati was shocked by the antics of the satirical Society for the Suppression of Music. *From* Cincinnati Commercial, *March 6, 1880.*

a letter read at an early meeting: "I have in my home an instrument of torture known as a piano. My sister performs upon the same, likewise my wife. Where are the liberties guaranteed to us by the Constitution of the United States and the State of Ohio? Something will come of this. I hope it mayn't be human gore."

The fulminations of the society led the *Cincinnati Gazette* to editorialize:

The fact that nearly every house has a piano is alleged as proof that we are a musical people, whereas these pianos are in general proof that our citizens have no musical sensations or possibilities. There ought to be a 4ᵗʰ of July bonfire of pianos; it would be a greater relief than the Declaration of Independence.

At one meeting, the society heard a letter suggesting specific punishments for musical infractions:

Any man, woman or child over two years, caught whistling in the streets should be marched to the nearest glass factory and be made to blow for a living. Piano pounders should be forced to wear boxing gloves and give security to keep them on during the pleasure of the Mayor. The musical critic, who in describing an opera or a concert, writes one word more than the Chief of Police, or, in his absence, the Chief of the Fire Department can understand with the assistance of the Wharf Master, shall be taken to the largest establishment where boilers are knocked into shape, and be made to explain Wagner's music of the future amid the clash of hammers and roar of riveters.

Although the society was active at the time the May Festival was in flower, the College of Music was being founded and Music Hall was under construction, the citizens appeared to take the lampooning of the society in stride.

Newspaper reports of society shenanigans were often accompanied by a reproduction of the society's insignia, depicting a man with an axe attacking a pile of musical instruments. Although later reports attribute the design to Judge Nicholas Longworth, it is almost certain that—whoever developed the concept—the execution was Farny's.

DR. OSLER'S FATAL JOKE

Some Cincinnati humor was much darker. Both Monty Python and Al Capp's Li'l Abner comic have explored the concept of a joke so hilarious that anyone who heard it would die laughing. Jokesters would have loved Dr. William Osler. He once told a joke that really did kill people, including some in Cincinnati.

For a respected medical authority, Dr. Osler was quite the comedian. Under the pseudonym of Egerton Yorrick Davis, he mailed bogus research papers to distinguished scientific journals, which often published them. These fake articles usually involved gynecological or urological topics that were decidedly off-color. Osler's most controversial joke was intended as self-deprecating humor. When it backfired, he spent the rest of his life trying to undo the damage.

It all began in 1905, when Oxford University in England invited Osler, one of the founders of Johns Hopkins Hospital in Baltimore, to accept a distinguished professorship in medicine. Osler was fifty-six years old and, in a farewell speech to his Johns Hopkins colleagues, suggested modestly that his best years were behind him. According to the *Cincinnati Enquirer* of February 26, 1905, "Not everybody understands so easily the professor's parting joke with his old associates at Baltimore. Some people have taken seriously his solemn protestation that at 40 a man is comparatively useless, while at 60 he should be unobtrusively chloroformed."

Problem is, although the newspapers reported it that way, that is not what Osler actually said. While he definitely stated his belief that men accomplish their best work before the age of sixty, Osler's comments regarding chloroform were quoted from British novelist Anthony Trollope. The Washington, D.C. *Evening Star* of February 23, 1905, published a verbatim transcript of Osler's speech: "In that charming novel, 'The Fixed Period,' Anthony Trollope discusses the practical advantages in modern life of a return to this ancient usage, and the plot hinges on the admirable scheme of a college into which at sixty men retired for a year of peaceful contemplation before a peaceful departure by chloroform."

Although Osler jokingly endorsed the general concept, he credited that satirical novel as the source. This nuance was lost on the mass media, and headlines across the United States claimed that a top medical doctor recommended a peaceful death by chloroform for men over age sixty. Some Cincinnati readers agreed and promptly killed themselves. On August 21, 1908, the *Post* reported, "No less than 10 men and women over the age of 60 have taken their own lives in Cincinnati during the past year. Nearly all of these believed they had reached their limit of usefulness, in line with this theory supposed to have been advanced by Dr. Osler."

The *Post* quoted an aged Cincinnati veteran who had retired to the Dayton Soldiers Home. Just before he killed himself, he supposedly told his acquaintances, "Dr. Osler is right. I am too old to be of any use to mankind."

One decided skeptic about Osler's influence was Dr. Otis L. Cameron, coroner of Hamilton County. While Dr. Cameron absolved Dr. Osler, he hardly offered a ray of hope for the county's elderly. He told the *Cincinnati Post*, "Dr. Osler never uttered it and I have never taken it seriously. It may have had some effect on old people. As a rule, however, they have other mighty good reasons for taking their own lives."

Well, thank you for the encouragement, Dr. Cameron!

SUICIDE BY LYSOL

For some Cincinnatians, there was no solace either among the Theosophists, spiritualists or mainstream religions. During the 1800s, suicide was common in Cincinnati and often involved drinking carbolic acid, a phenolic compound used as a disinfectant. In the early 1900s, however, carbolic acid was essentially replaced by Lysol disinfectant. Lysol was first sold in Germany in 1889. Among the ingredients of early Lysol formulations were benzalkonium chloride and some organic compounds called cresols (a type of phenol), both poisonous in significant quantities.

As early as 1894, medical authorities in Germany had estimated that one hundred suicides each year in Germany were caused by a product just five years on the market. A single neighborhood in Berlin yielded twenty-four suicides by Lysol that year. By 1913, Lysol was the most popular means of suicide in Germany and Australia. Cincinnatians followed suit. The Cincinnati birth and death records housed at the University of Cincinnati archives record at least eight suicides between 1905 and 1914 involving Lysol ingestion, all involving women. Men, then as now, most often resorted to firearms and hanging to end their lives.

THE DEATH FAMILY

After absorbing all of these insights into Cincinnati's weird history, it will not surprise you to learn that Death, himself, once resided in our fair city. He was a most respectable citizen and held some distinguished public appointments. Absalom Death was a doctor and professor of medicine, ran the Cincinnati Commercial Hospital and was prominent in the city's Masonic lodge. He was married, and so there was an entire family of Deaths in residence among our citizenry. The Death family lived on Western Row in the 1850s. Perhaps

Mr. Absalom Death, despite his grim cognomen and baleful mien, was a popular and respected official in early Cincinnati. *University of Cincinnati Archives.*

the most macabre name in the annals of Cincinnati, and certainly the most goth, belongs to a daughter of this family, Miss Arachne Death.

Arachne's father was named Absalom Death, and he sold rectified whiskey. Almost all Cincinnati whiskey back in the day fell into a mysterious category called "rectified whiskey." An imbiber named William Smith remembered this concoction:

> *Some of these were compounds that were termed—with no excuse whatever—"rectified whiskey." Such compounds often consisted of alcohol, distilled water, burnt sugar for coloring, bead oil, and rye or bourbon flavoring. In rare cases in which the compounder was squeamish or even honest, a modicum of good whiskey was added, assisted by a little glycerine or castor oil to take the scratch out of the alcohol.*

Over his shop on Main Street, Absalom Death had a sign that read "Rectified Whiskey," and underneath that was his name. One day, a near-sighted woman from the country rode by Mr. Death's establishment in her son's carriage. Upon misreading the sign, she called out to the young man and ordered him to stop immediately. "Rectified Whiskey! Absolute Death! That's a fact. Johnny, let me get out. There is at least one honest man in Cincinnati, and I want to see what he looks like!"

Chapter 2

THE DEAD BENEATH OUR FEET

Cincinnati is not unique in claiming to be situated on seven hills, but we are unusual in that we have consistently failed to specify precisely which of our so-called hills compose this canonical septet. Before we consider the hills themselves, we must peer into the wonderful bedrock from which they were sculpted, for Cincinnati has a bedrock foundation unlike any city in the world.

Daniel Drake, pioneer physician, claimed that our geology affected our health and touted our "hard" water, chockfull of minerals, as a natural tonic for New Englanders raised on wimpy "soft" water. To the contrary, a local geologist named John Lea blamed Cincinnati's mortality during the 1849 cholera epidemic on the dearth of metallic salts in our local bedrock.

During the Ordovician Period, 450 million years ago, when our limestones were precipitating from the ancient waters, cholera remedies awaited a far distant future. Cincinnati lay at the bottom of a shallow sea, teeming with marine life, some as familiar as coral, some extinct like the trilobites. Their fossilized remains are so famous that geologists refer to the period when our local rocks and fossils were deposited as the Cincinnatian Epoch.

As the Ordovician seas rose and fell, they left behind alternating layers of limestone and softer shale. Commuters navigating the I-75 "Cut in the Hill" in northern Kentucky can view a dramatic example of these "layer-cake" deposits on the adjacent hillside.

Cincinnati's limestones are rock-solid and constitute the many fieldstone walls that line our more venerable streets. Those stones, despite the name,

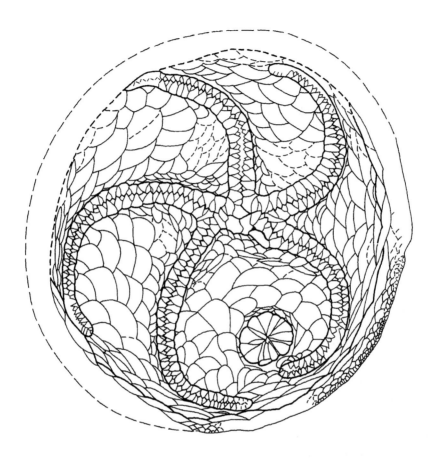

Isorophus cincinnatiensis was fairly common in the shallow seas that covered Cincinnati 450 million years ago. It is now Cincinnati's official fossil. *Cincinnati Dry Dredgers*.

did not come from any field. Quarries atop Price Hill, Mount Auburn and Fairview churned out native building stone for a century or more.

Our shale, on the other hand, turns into a slippery, oleaginous muck when saturated with rainwater. Because of this lubrication, Cincinnati has the highest per-capita damage from landslides of any city in the United States. Paleontologists, a contrary bunch, appreciate a good landslide because it exposes new specimens, and Cincinnati's offerings are treasured around the world. No respectable natural history museum considers its collections complete without some representative samples of Cincinnati fossils.

Few American cities claim their very own official fossil, but Cincinnati does. Quarter-sized *Isorophus cincinnatiensis* is an edrioasteroid, a relative of starfish. The fossil was named in honor of our city in the 1840s by a German scientist, and in 2002, the Queen City returned the favor by voting the extinct little critter into certified status.

Although Cincinnati's geologic wonders are among the most intensely studied rocks and fossils in the world, they still yield shocking discoveries. In 2010, amateur paleontologist Ron Fine discovered an enigmatic and previously undescribed fossil of a seven-foot-tall organism just across the river in Covington. Fine describes the creature, dubbed Godzillus, as resembling a saguaro cactus with flattened branches and horizontal stripes in place of the usual vertical stripes. Scientists are still debating just how to classify the huge and enigmatic creature.

Even larger than Godzillus, Cincinnati's rocks remember the tracks of Ordovician storms. It was, after all, a tropical sea, and our hills actually preserve the fossilized remnants of 450-million-year-old hurricanes.

CINCINNATI'S SEVEN (OR SEVENTY-FIVE) HILLS

Julia Lee Sinks remembered Cincinnati's hills. In 1897, the *Cincinnati Enquirer* sent a reporter out to Giddings, Texas, to inquire about Sinks's Cincinnati childhood. At the age of eighty, she was an established historian of her adopted state. But she was born and raised in Cincinnati, and she remembered the hills:

> *In memory I still stand on a little cricket stool at the front window of a plain brick dwelling looking out at the hills, which environed the city of Cincinnati. No pagan worshipped his idols with more love than did this little girl the three grand hills, as they seem now: Lytle's, over Deercreek; Dickinson's, over Millcreek, in Delhi Township, and Key's, over which then one of the main thoroughfares led.*

A modern reader will not recognize the names of any of these hills. Today, each is known by a totally different name. Lytle's Hill is now known as Mount Adams. Dickinson's Hill is now Price Hill. Key's Hill is now Mount Auburn.

Most Cincinnatians remember that Mount Adams was renamed to honor U.S. president John Quincy Adams in 1843. Prior to that, the hill was known variously as Lytle Hill (according to Sinks) and Mount Ida for reasons that are more legendary than factual. An 1841 magazine records another nickname for Mount Adams: Waterworks Hill.

Looming around the Cincinnati downtown, our hills are an essential aspect of our geography. But how many hills are there? *From Charles Cist,* Sketches and Statistics of Cincinnati in 1859.

As for Dickinson's Hill, those of us who lived through the 1960s remember a running gag on radio station WEBN, then located on Considine Avenue in Price Hill. The DJ regularly announced the station's location as "Price's Mountain." Despite that intended ostentation, Price Hill was in fact known throughout the 1800s as "Price's Hill." The possessive referenced the eccentric landowner Reese Price, who occupied the summit of that hill and paid for the incline that ran up from Eighth Street. What is not so well remembered is that Price's Hill did not cover the entirety of what we now call Price Hill.

According to old maps, "Price's Hill" referred only to the slope on which the incline ran, the area now called the Incline District. What we call Price Hill today included four other hills whose names are almost lost to history. Beginning at the southern side of today's Price Hill we had Mount Echo, memorialized in Mount Echo Park, offering perhaps the most picturesque view of our city from the west. A little behind Mount Echo, southwest of Enright Avenue, is Mount Hope. But the largest of Price Hill's hills was Mount Harrison, which rises nearly 870 feet high a block north of the old WEBN studio location on Considine Avenue.

Mount Auburn was known as Key's Hill after an early landowner named James Key. That all changed in 1837, when a New England lady enamored of British poetry arrived for a visit and found the residents debating a new name for their neighborhood. The visitor resolved the debate by placing a sign, inspired by Oliver Goldsmith's poem "Sweet Auburn," along the Carthage Pike that said "One Mile to Mount Auburn."

All of which raises an essential question: what are Cincinnati's seven hills? The short answer is, it depends on who you ask. The very first attempt to list Cincinnati's hills was by George W.L. Bickley in the June 1853 issue of his magazine, *Bickley's West American Review*. He listed Mount Adams, Walnut Hills, Mount Auburn, Vine Street Hill, College Hill, Fairmount and Mount Harrison. Since Bickley, various attempts to name Cincinnati's hills have resulted in counts ranging from zero (on the theory Cincinnati has no hills, only valleys) to something like seventy-five individually named slopes. The most common candidates are Mount Adams, Mount Auburn, Mount Harrison or Price Hill, Walnut Hills, Fairmount, Mount Lookout, Mount Echo, Clifton Heights, Fairview Heights, Mount Hope, Vine Street Hill, Clifton, College Hill, Mount Airy, Mount Healthy, Mount Storm, Mount Washington and Tusculum, in more or less that order.

THE LONG-LOST PREHISTORIC MOUNDS OF DOWNTOWN CINCINNATI

Not counted among that number today, because they have all been demolished, are the extensive man-made hills left behind by the Mound Builders. Nothing remains of them today except Mound Street's name, but when European settlers first arrived, the whole flat plain of Cincinnati's "basin" was overspread with prehistoric earthworks, including walls and burial mounds. The ancient structures were visible even though the area was heavily wooded. William Henry Harrison, as a young officer at Fort Washington, participated in a survey of these mounds, accompanying General "Mad" Anthony Wayne. Years later, in an 1837 address to the Historical and Philosophical Society of Ohio, he recalled:

> When I first saw the upper plain on which that city stands, it was literally covered with low lines of embankments. I had the honor to attend General Wayne two years afterwards in an excursion to examine them. We were employed a greater part of a day, in August, 1793, in doing so. The number and variety of figures in which these lines were drawn, was almost endless, and, as I have said, almost covered the plain.

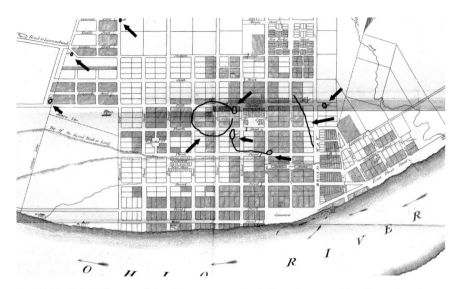

Daniel Drake's 1815 map of the downtown area includes a dozen prehistoric earthworks that were demolished as the city grew. *From Daniel Drake,* Picture of Cincinnati, *1815.*

It's among the most hackneyed plots in horror films, but everyone knows nothing good comes from building on top of an Indian graveyard. That, however, is exactly what Cincinnati's settlers did. Many of Cincinnati's conical mounds were proven during their destruction to have been burial monuments containing beads, tools, shells and minerals, in addition to human remains.

Daniel Drake, in his 1815 *Natural and Statistical View,* or *Picture of Cincinnati,* drew the locations of some of the major earthworks on a map included with his book. In the text, Drake describes these "Antient works," although he was at a loss to say who built them.

We now know that the mounds and other earthworks were, indeed, the creation of the ancestors of the American Indians. Most of the Cincinnati earthworks were from the Adena culture, which flourished in the Ohio River Valley from 1000 BC to 200 BC, so they were at least two thousand years old when William Henry Harrison first saw them.

CINCINNATI IS JUST ONE BIG GRAVEYARD

Having obliterated the Adena burial mounds, Cincinnati began creating thousands of new graveyards and then promptly forgot about them as our residents migrated and engaged in urban renewal projects. Many of these old burials were relocated to Spring Grove Cemetery after 1845, but certainly not all of them.

Dig almost anywhere around the city, and there is a good chance you'll find human remains. As Cincinnati grew, burial grounds located way out on the outskirts of town got swallowed up by encroaching development. Sometimes, new buildings were erected atop old cemeteries without even moving the bodies.

Most Cincinnatians know about the skeletons discovered during the renovation of Music Hall. That iconic structure was built atop the old Potter's Field. Across Elm Street, Washington Park occupies land once used as two "burying grounds," one for Presbyterians and the other for Episcopalians.

The oldest recorded burial in Cincinnati took place in 1764—nearly a quarter-century before the first settlers arrived here in 1788. The discovery of this skeleton was a curious coincidence according to A.E. Jones, author of *Extracts from the History of Cincinnati* (1888), who describes an old man sitting on the veranda of the Old Red Tavern, located just about where Suspension Bridge now anchors to the north shore of the Ohio River. As he watched some workmen digging a trench on the riverbank, the old man got up and ambled over.

> *Leaning upon his cane, he asked what they were digging for. They told him they were making a drain. "Well," said he, after looking over at Licking and all around him, as if getting the points of the compass. "Within six feet of where you are digging there is a man buried," and pointing with his cane said, "Dig right there and you will find it; if it is not rotten, you will find a bullet hole over the right eye." Rather to gratify the old man, than from any confidence in what he said, they dug where he had indicated, and sure enough, about three feet underground they found the skeleton, and the bullet hole over the right eye, in the skull; and the ball rattled in the skull when they pulled it up.*

It turns out the elderly gentleman was a British soldier in 1764, some sixty years earlier, and had camped with his patrol on that exact spot when they were attacked by Indians in league with the French. One of his comrades fell dead and was hastily buried as the patrol made their escape.

That is hardly the only example of new construction displacing old graves. A brief squib in the August 22, 1851 *Cincinnati Enquirer* notes that "the old burying ground in the rear of the College building" between Fourth and

Once Spring Grove Cemetery was opened in 1845, some old cemeteries were emptied and the remains transferred there. *Library of Congress.*

Fifth had been sold to a developer who planned to erect a row of warehouses. Those buildings were later demolished and newer buildings constructed. According to the October 23, 1910 *Cincinnati Post*, many of the new buildings had curious souvenirs hidden in their basements or back rooms:

> *Israel Ludlow, who platted Cincinnati, was buried in the rear of the building on Fourth-st., near Walnut, now occupied by Julius Baer's floral store. A tablet erected to his memory is still standing in the rear of Baer's store....Headstones of other pioneer Cincinnatians buried in the Fourth-st. block, which was used as a graveyard early in the Nineteenth Century, are still standing in the rear yards of other business houses in the square.*

Skeletons have been found all over town. When the old Fourteenth District School at the corner of Poplar and Freeman was torn down to build what later became the old Sands Montessori building, a child's coffin was dug up by workmen excavating the foundation. According to the *Post* of March 14, 1911, "The lot on which the school was situated and on which the new school is to be built, is supposed to contain many coffins and bones. The Fourteenth District School was an old structure when it was torn down. It is supposed to have been built on an abandoned graveyard."

When an insurance executive named Elliott Marfield built a mansion along Vernon Avenue near Oak Street (approximately where the Vernon Manor is located today) in 1895, workers dug up eight or ten skeletons. Some were still quite identifiable. They had been interred in an abandoned German Protestant cemetery.

Until 1905, the lot at the corner of Madison and Erie in Hyde Park was used as a graveyard, according to the *Cincinnati Post* of June 30, 1905: "The fact that it was formerly a graveyard will not interfere with its use as a city park, however."

The *Cincinnati Commercial Gazette* of April 21, 1889, reported multiple skeletons in various stages of preservation when a subdivision was carved into the hills west of what is now Virginia Avenue in Northside. One skeleton was almost seven feet tall.

When Ashland Avenue was extended in Walnut Hills, quite a number of old caskets got dug up. The *Cincinnati Post* of April 20, 1894, noted, "The street runs through what once was an old graveyard, but which has been forgotten for many years. Older residents say that the burial place was known as the old English Graveyard. Two iron caskets, of oval bowl shape, were turned up by the plows."

The entire block where Hays-Porter Elementary School is located was once two burial grounds, one for Protestants and one for Catholics. As early as 1886, workmen dug up nearly two dozen skulls and associated bones while preparing a cellar.

In 1911, Delhi Township held an auction to sell an old graveyard along Neeb Road. Since it was adjacent to the old Meyers No. 3 District Schoolhouse, the local school board bought it for use as a playground. Trampled by decades of young schoolchildren, this old boneyard now lies beneath the campus of Mount St. Joseph University.

And in South Cumminsville, the wooded area south of Wayne Playground, where Dreman Avenue crosses the West Fork of the Mill Creek, was once the Friends Burial Ground. It fell out of use so long ago that a 1900 newspaper story says it was abandoned and used as a cow pasture.

CINCINNATI'S NOTORIOUS GHOUL

It is amazing that anything remains in these old graveyards, since Cincinnati was once plagued by an army of grave robbers, the most infamous of whom was William Cunningham. While he was alive, Cincinnatians called him

"Old Man Dead" or "Old Cunny" and invoked his name to frighten naughty children, but in 1872, he was nothing but a skeleton on view at the Medical College of Ohio. The *Enquirer* noted that the only accoutrements missing from this grisly exhibit were Cunningham's gray horse and spring wagon because Old Man Dead was a ghoul, a body snatcher, a grave robber. His skeleton was on exhibit at the medical college because he wanted it that way. He sold his own body to the Medical College of Ohio for fifty dollars, and after their students were done practicing on it, the faculty had the skeleton arranged in this macabre tableau.

Old Cunny died on November 2, 1871, and hard living had prematurely aged him. The coroner estimated his age as sixty-five, but he claimed to be just fifty years old when the United States census enumerator knocked on his door the year before he died. Cunningham told the census taker that he drove an express wagon. That's how he listed his occupation in the city directory as well. Maybe he did make some express deliveries in the warm-weather months.

When the first frosts nipped the graveyard air, Old Cunny harvested bodies from cemeteries all over the Cincinnati area. In Cunningham's heyday, Cincinnati had multiple medical schools. Each had dozens to hundreds of students, and all needed cadavers to study anatomy. Cunningham and his competitors provided the bodies.

Old Cunny made a very vivid impression, indeed, on a clerk at the American Express office when he showed up with a box marked "Glass. Handle with Care" and addressed to a Dr. Hardy in Leavenworth, Kansas. Old Cunny wanted the box sent COD (collect on delivery), with the thirty-dollar fee returned to him. As Cunningham drove off, the clerk acted on his suspicions and opened the box. Sure enough, the corpse of a woman was inside, hastily embalmed and packed in sawdust, doubled up in a canvas sack.

Despite some buckshot in his leg, Cunningham got away with more "resurrections" than not. A "very knowing acquaintance" told this tale to the *Enquirer* on March 1, 1874, after Cunningham's death:

> One night, I remember, I met Cunny driving into the city with a stiff; and, horrible as the sight was, there was something grotesquely ludicrous about it. He had placed the corpse in a sitting posture on the seat beside him, and had dressed it in an old coat and a vest and a played out hat. Well he kept his arm round the waist of the corpse to steady it from the jolting of the vehicle. But every now and then the horrid thing would double up on the

seat, and its head kept bobbing up and down in the ghastliest way you ever saw. Then Old Cunny would give the stiff a slap in the face and say: "Sit up; this is the last time, by God, I'll ever take you home when you get drunk. You ought to be ashamed of yourself—drunker'n a biled owl—with a wife and children to support."

Chapter 3

TALES FROM THE OLD CITY

Today, Cincinnati loves its flying pigs, a fantasy creature based on our heritage as a pork-packing powerhouse. Few contemporary Cincinnatians can conceive of the pungent reality of Porkopolis back in the days when slurping, grunting, reeking swine infested every yard and alley. According to Moses King in his 1879 *Pocket-Book of Cincinnati*, our city's nickname began in England:

> *Porkopolis is one of the names by which Cincinnati is known, and its origin is explained in the following manner: About 1825 George W. Jones, president of the United States branch-bank, and known as "Bank Jones," was very enthusiastic about the fact that 25,000 to 30,000 hogs were being killed in this city every year; and in his letters to the bank's Liverpool correspondent he never failed to mention the fact, and express his hope of Cincinnati's future greatness as a provision-market. The correspondent, after receiving a number of these letters, had a unique pair of model hogs made of papier-mâché, and sent them to George W. Jones as the worthy representative of "Porkopolis."*

Cincinnati's pork production was a winter industry. Only cold temperatures adequately chilled the butchered hogs throughout the slaughtering, chopping and packing process. Industrial freezers would not become economical until long after Chicago had usurped Cincinnati's former role as "hog butcher to the world." During the summer, a visitor to Cincinnati would have no idea why the town was called Porkopolis.

Few recall that Cincinnati did not acquire its nickname of Porkopolis as a compliment. *From Harper's Weekly, February 4, 1860.*

Come autumn, however, visitors found porcine evidence all around them, whether they wanted to or not. Frances "Fanny" Trollope is infamous for publishing a scathing indictment of Cincinnati in her 1832 book *Domestic Manners of the Americans*:

> *If I determined upon a walk up Main-street, the chances were five hundred to one against my reaching the shady side without brushing by a snout fresh dipping from the kennel; when we had screwed our courage to the enterprise of mounting a certain noble-looking sugar-loaf hill, that promised pure air and a fine view, we found the brook we had to cross, at its foot, red with the stream from a pig slaughterhouse while our noses, instead of meeting "the thyme that loves the green hill's breast," were greeted by odours that I will not describe, and which I heartily hope my readers cannot imagine.*

And Fanny wrote when Cincinnati was only just beginning its long run to pork-packing prominence. In 1856, another Englishwoman, Isabella Lucy Bird, came to town and had many nice things to say in her book *The Englishwoman in America*:

But after describing the beauty of her streets, her astonishing progress, and the splendour of her shops, I must not close this chapter without stating that the Queen City bears the less elegant name of Porkopolis; that swine, lean, gaunt, and vicious looking, riot through her streets; and that, on coming out of the most splendid stores, one stumbles over these disgusting intruders. Cincinnati is the city of pigs. As there is a railway system and a hotel system, so there is also a pig system by which this place is marked out from any other. At a particular time of year they arrive by thousands—brought in droves and steamers to the number of 500,000—to meet their doom, when it is said that the Ohio runs red with blood.

In 1860, at the height of Cincinnati's dominance of the industry, pigs had taken over the city. Here is Nicholas Augustus Woods, special correspondent to the *Times* of London:

They pervade the whole place—the very gutters are congested with them, and a sort of dull monotony of pigs is visible everywhere. They come against you wherever you turn, from huge, black, muddy, unsightly monsters, down to little sucklings not much bigger than kittens, on which you inadvertently tread and stumble, amid shrill squeakings almost enough to blow you off your legs, and quite enough to alarm the neighbourhood, if it had not long ago got used to every possible variation of noise in which swine can convey their thrilling protests of resentment or alarm.

Thank heavens, indeed, that pigs cannot fly!

THE PLAGUE SPOT

Pigs were not the only source of offensive odors in Porkopolis. By the 1860s, nearly 200,000 people called Cincinnati home. Most of those inhabitants were packed into the downtown basin between the river and the surrounding hills, and all of them had to poop.

At the time, indoor plumbing was almost nonexistent. Sewers were an expensive innovation just beginning to catch on. Most Cincinnatians relieved themselves in unheated outhouses tucked away at the back of the property where they lived, and all of those outhouses perched over a deep and smelly pit known as a privy vault. The situation was every bit as disgusting as you can imagine. The *Cincinnati Commercial Tribune* of May 23, 1859, opined:

We have time and again warned the public of the danger accruing from dilapidated out-houses, beneath the worm eaten floors of which yawn the disgusting receptacle of a privy vault. Hardly a week elapses, that we are not called upon to chronicle some accident arising from the insecurity of these dreadful pit-traps, which should be subjected to the periodical examination of some competent person.

In fact, there was such a competent person, and his name was William Clendenin. He was Cincinnati's health officer, and he fulfilled the happy profession of inspecting the city's privy vaults. The *Cincinnati Gazette* of April 30, 1866, carried Clendenin's report to the city's Health Commission, in which he noted, "About 830 privy vaults have been inspected; and up to the present time nearly 50 per cent of all those examined were either full and emitting noisome odors, or needed repairs and cleaning."

In other words, most of Cincinnati's privy vaults leaked raw sewage onto the ground, into the street or, worst of all, into neighboring houses. One such vault afflicted Bernard O'Brien, living near the intersection of Sycamore

The outhouse or privy served the bathroom needs in some Cincinnati neighborhoods well into the 1950s. *Library of Congress.*

and Eighth Streets. He brought suit against his neighbors whose privy vault was in bad repair, alleging that the contents ran into his cellar, causing an intolerable nuisance.

The *Commercial Tribune* estimated that someone died about once a week by falling into a privy vault. The old newspapers are full of such incidents, often involving children who tumbled to their doom. Men suffocated from the fumes while cleaning or repairing vaults. Sometimes drunks leaned a little too far over. The worst disaster in this region occurred in 1904, when a rotten floor gave way and nine young girls dropped into a privy vault and died at Pleasant Ridge School.

By law, Cincinnati's privy vaults were deep. The law required a minimum of twenty feet, but if the excavation had not reached sand or gravel at that level, it needed to be six feet deeper. Commercial pits, like those attached to factories and businesses, reached even farther underground. For example, the privy vault at the Bremen Street police station was sixty feet deep.

Even so, the vaults filled up and needed to be emptied from time to time. The entrepreneurs who engaged in this repulsive occupation were euphemistically known as the "night-cart brigade," driving their "honey wagons" from privy to privy. The Cincinnati night carts were leaky and odiferous and trundled over cobblestone streets slopping unimaginable filth with every bump. Where did they dump these loads of excrement? Usually into the Ohio River or, if they were lazy, into the Miami Canal. Sometimes they only hauled their foul cargo a couple of blocks away and dumped it into the nearest gutter.

Even after the city began installing functional underground sewers, few people used them. By 1870, when Cincinnati had a total population of 216,238, there were only 671 officially recorded house connections.

Twelve years later, there was still room for improvement. In 1882, a sewer inspector named W.H. Baldwin visited Cincinnati on behalf of the United States Census Bureau. Baldwin spent six weeks studying Cincinnati's growing sewer system and found it very impressive. On his way out of town, however, he left a warning, as reported in the *Commercial Tribune* of January 27, 1882:

> *Mr. Baldwin reports that the sewerage of Cincinnati will compare favorably with that of any other large city, but he announces the rather startling fact that a plague spot is generating in the heart of the city, from the fact that in the large area extending from Broadway to Freeman and from Court to the Hills with a population of 80,000 people, only about 30,000 use the*

sewers for house drainage, and the water closets of the remaining 50,000 being sunk in the ground only the liquid deposit is absorbed, leaving the solid matter to accumulate to such an extent that it is only a question of time how soon "earth-poisoning" and pestilence will arouse the authorities to the fact "that something must be done."

Very little, in fact, was done. As late as 1952, the *Cincinnati Enquirer* reported, "A typical family living in Cincinnati's basin occupies two rooms, uses an outdoor toilet with other families, has no hot water or central heating."

Mrs. Trollope Scandalizes Cincinnati

One author, whose aversion to swine has been briefly mentioned, deserves a closer look because of her significant impact on our city.

Frances Milton Trollope, known as "Fanny," was English, and she married unwisely. Thomas A. Trollope was a renowned lawyer who had no clients because he disagreed with all of them. Fanny Trollope seems to have disagreed with everyone else. It was a marriage made somewhere other than heaven. Mr. and Mrs. Trollope built one of those uniquely British mansions on leased land in full anticipation of an inheritance from an elderly and widowed uncle. The uncle had other ideas, remarried in his dotage and was blessed by a May-December heir. The Trollopes were ruined.

In desperation, Mrs. Trollope lit out for the colonies along with half of her offspring, a manservant and (but of course!) a threadbare French artist named Jean Jacques Auguste Hervieu. After an initial stop at the obvious source of American riches—a free-thinking commune in the backwoods of Tennessee—Fanny et al. lit out for civilization. Cincinnati would never be the same.

She arrived in Cincinnati in 1828 and attached herself to the fledgling Western Museum, a struggling if not quite bankrupt business enterprise. A core collection of fossils, archaeological artifacts and botanical and mineral specimens had been industriously augmented by the efforts of naturalist John James Audubon and preserved by curator Joseph Dorfeuille. The public was bored and absent, except for that one evening when a museum-sponsored lecture on laughing gas was accompanied by free samples.

What Dorfeuille needed was a truly eccentric Englishwoman. Fanny Trollope arrived as if on cue. She enlisted her household artist, Hervieu, to help a future sculpture superstar named Hiram Powers conjure a lurid

Fanny Trollope holds court while her personal artist, Auguste Hervieu, paints a scene. *Library of Congress.*

exposition of Dante's *Divine Comedy*, emphasizing the horrors of Hell. Cincinnati was all about horrors, diabolical or otherwise, and the infernal bowels of the Western Museum became the city's hot ticket.

Giddy with success, Mrs. Trollope was inspired to greater heights. She intended, among other things, to remake the entire Cincinnati skyline. Cincinnati lacked domes, Mrs. Trollope decreed, so she built her Bazaar to supply one and to make her fortune.

Four floors tall, capped by the incongruous "Moorish-Arabesque" dome, forty feet wide by one hundred feet long, the Bazaar dominated Third Street. It was a sort of department store, true, but the building also housed an art and exhibition gallery, ballroom, barroom and two salons for theatrical presentations and literary gatherings. The building's heating fixtures spewed miasmas reminiscent of Fanny's hellish tableaux at the museum. The heating was uncontrollable, and the lighting belched noxious fumes. As a commercial establishment, the Bazaar was a nightmare. Fanny stocked the shelves with cheap European junk no one would buy and locally purchased stock, outrageously marked up, that everyone had already bought elsewhere.

Bankrupt once again, Mrs. Trollope retreated to England and licked her wounds by writing *Domestic Manners of the Americans* (1832) about the manners of those backward Americans—especially Cincinnatians. The book told all, named names, scandalized a continent and sold out over several editions. Mrs. Trollope had at last earned her fortune.

And the Third Street Bazaar? It had numerous and curious lives. From time to time, the Bazaar building was an inn, a ballroom, a church, a theater, a hospital, a bordello, an eclectic medical school and the home of the Ohio Mechanics Institute.

AARON BURR'S SECOND ACT

THE LITTLE MAN IN BLACK.

Aaron Burr in caricature, illustrating a short story by Washington Irving, "The Little Man in Black." *Library of Congress.*

Another visitor to early Cincinnati was the notorious traitor Aaron Burr.

Now that everyone has watched Lin-Manuel Miranda's *Hamilton: An American Musical*, it might be appropriate to propose a sequel that follows Aaron Burr to Cincinnati, where he treasonously plotted against the United States—because that is pretty much what he did.

Politically ruined as the murderer of Alexander Hamilton, Burr hatched a plot to restore his reputation and his fortune by snatching the Louisiana Purchase away from the United States, grabbing most of the northern Mexico territory and creating an empire with himself as emperor. Burr's plan was to magnify some minor border disputes between the United States and Spain into a full-blown revolution against Spanish occupation, with Burr playing the George Washington role.

In his efforts to put this scheme in motion while not arousing suspicion, Burr made multiple trips up and down the Ohio and Mississippi Rivers between 1805 and 1807. It is a matter of record that Burr passed through

Cincinnati several times as he knitted together the disparate threads of his plot and spent most of those visits at the Terrace Park home of Ohio's first senator, John Smith. Elder Smith, as he was known, was a Baptist preacher who arrived providentially in the Ohio River town of Columbia right after the only minister in town fled the frontier and returned east. Smith led the little church while building up a lucrative business selling provisions to the army, first at Fort Washington in Cincinnati and then throughout Kentucky and the Northwest Territory.

When Ohio was carved out of the Northwest Territory to become the seventeenth state in 1803, Elder Smith was appointed to represent the new state in the United States Senate. The vice president at the time was Aaron Burr, who in that role served as president of the Senate. Smith and Burr got along famously, and Smith continued to support Burr even after the fatal duel with Hamilton.

It is known that Burr entrusted Smith with large sums of conspiratorial cash, which Smith dispersed on Burr's instructions to active participants in the conspiracy. It is known that Smith knew Burr's whereabouts and kept this intelligence confidential.

On the other hand, Smith, in apparent innocence, wrote to Burr to inquire if the rumors of traitorous conspiracy were true. Burr responded by fiercely denying the allegations. Nevertheless, after Burr's plot imploded, John Quincy Adams introduced a resolution recommending Smith's expulsion from the Senate because of his association with Burr. The measure failed to gather enough votes, but Smith knew his clout had evaporated and resigned from the Senate.

Senator John Smith is all but forgotten, except for two Cincinnati streets. Today, there is only a nubbin left of Smith Street, running west of the Clay Wade Bailey Bridge ramp, and John Street, from Court north to York in the West End, is barely noticed by commuters these days. Both of these once-proud streets were named for Ohio's first and disgraced senator, John Smith, the host of traitor Aaron Burr.

THE GALLOWS ON GOVERNMENT SQUARE

Had Burr been convicted, he might have faced punishment right here in Cincinnati. Public executions were a popular spectacle here for many years.

Cincinnati sheriff John Ludlow hanged James Mays on October 26, 1792, from gallows erected on Fifth Street a little east of Walnut. According to Charles Greve's *Centennial History of Cincinnati*, the hanging on the south side of what is now Government Square was a popular spectacle: "The execution was public, as all such affairs were at that time, and the people gathered from every direction to see it. Excursions were brought into the city and many came as far as fifty miles to be present."

Mays earned the distinction of being the first civilian executed in Hamilton County by stabbing his friend Matthew Sullivan during a drunken argument. Although the first civilian, Mays was not the first local execution. William L. DeBeck, in his anonymously published book *Murder Will Out*, credits the U.S. Army, based at Fort Washington, with sentencing some deserters to death by firing squad.

Cincinnati's pioneers witnessed a fair number of executions and other public punishments. In its early days, Cincinnati didn't even have a proper courthouse. According to pioneer citizen Jacob Burnet, trials were conducted in a tavern at the corner of Main and Fifth Streets, and the yard outside was ornamented with a pillory, stocks, whipping post and, occasionally, gallows.

One early settler recalled the sheriff inflicting "forty stripes save one" on a woman convicted of setting fire to haystacks, while another recorded the same punishment applied to another woman guilty of theft. A man named Paddy Grimes earned twenty-nine lashes for stealing some vegetables. Sometimes, according to historian Charles Greve, sentences involved more than one punishment:

> *A discharged soldier, Peter Kerrigan, married Mary Murphy without publishing the banns; thereupon William Maxwell, the owner of the* Spy [Cincinnati's early newspaper], *who felt that he was entitled to the advertisement, caused him to be arrested and Peter received 10 stripes on the bare back and stood four hours in the public pillory and went to jail for three months.*

Even before Cincinnati had a proper courthouse, it had a jail. Most inmates were imprisoned for debt rather than criminal activity. The jail was run by a man named Levi McClean (or McLean), who was relatively indulgent unless he was in his cups. According to pioneer Samuel Stitt:

> *The first jail was on Water street, west of Main. It could be readily seen from the river. The debtors and criminals were all shut up together; but in daylight the jailer allowed them the liberty of the neighborhood, they taking care, whenever the sheriff was about, to make tracks to the jail as rats to*

their holes. There was a whipping-post, when I came to Cincinnati, about one hundred feet west of Main, and fifty feet south of Fifth street, near the line of Church alley. Levi McClean, the jailer, did the whipping. I saw a woman whipped for stealing. McClean would get drunk, at times, and in these frolics would amuse himself by whipping, with a cowhide, the prisoners in jail, all round, debtors as well as criminals.

Public hangings continued in Cincinnati until the 1880s. After that, punishment for capital offenses moved to the state penitentiary in Columbus.

THE NASTY CORNER

Although criminals were actually executed on Government Square, it was the southwest corner of Fifth and Vine Streets that became known as the "Nasty Corner." The *Cincinnati Commercial Gazette* of December 15, 1889, held its nose and opined:

There is no more prominently located spot in the city. It faces the widest part of Fifth Street and nearly all of the car lines of the city pass either close under its shadow or within a square of it. The Fountain is at its door and the ceaseless tides of Vine and Fifth streets mingle beneath its walls. For years it has been the eyesore to everyone who liked to see Cincinnati advance. It has been a synonym for all that is foul and unsightly. The visitor to the city has marveled at such squalor crouching in the middle of such opulence. People have passed by on the other side to avoid its stenches and unwashed loafers.

The Nasty Corner fell into decrepitude because the previous owner, David K. Este, died in 1876, leaving a great number of heirs who could not seem to agree on anything. In particular, they could not agree on what sort of building to construct on this increasingly valuable plot of downtown real estate.

The Nasty Corner is depicted in one of the most famous photographs of Cincinnati, often called the "Wienerwurst with Every Drink" photo. Often invoked to represent the Over-the-Rhine neighborhood, it actually illustrates Este's decrepit property.

The Nasty Corner finally surrendered to Joseph T. Carew, president of the Mabley & Carew department store. Carew built his store catty-corner to

"NASTY CORNER"—AN UGLY BLUR ON FOUNTAIN SQUARE.

The "Nasty Corner" blighted the busy intersection of Fifth and Vine for many years. *From Cincinnati Gazette, June 23, 1889.*

the Este block, giving him an exceptional view of the dilapidated buildings on the southwest corner.

Carew lobbied the Este heirs and convinced them to sign a deal on condition that he would build a brand-new and very impressive building on the Nasty Corner. And he did. The brand-new and very impressive Carew Building opened in 1891. Not quite forty years later, it was demolished to make way for the new Carew Tower, forever burying the old Nasty Corner.

Chapter 4

THE SENSATIONAL
AND THE SENSELESS

To demonstrate how intrinsically alien Cincinnati once was, let's drop in at the Palace Hotel on the night of Friday, December 12, 1890. On the menu is elephant steak. The Palace Hotel (today's Cincinnatian Hotel) has elephant steak on the menu because an elephant was executed by firing squad that morning at the Cincinnati Zoo. Hundreds of people watched. That pretty much summarizes Cincinnati in 1890.

Today, we have YouTube and Tik-Tok. Back then, Cincinnatians had to physically go someplace to see things, and Cincinnati residents thrived on sensational, tawdry, melodramatic and risqué entertainment just as we do today. Murdering an elephant was a guaranteed crowd pleaser.

How many marksmen does it take to kill an elephant? The Cincinnati Zoo needed two firing squads to execute Old Chief in 1890.

Chief was a murderer, true, but that was part of his allure. The zoo knew what it was getting when the John Robinson Circus convinced the zoo to take the cantankerous pachyderm off their hands. Chief was a big draw for a solid year at the zoo. A typical advertisement cajoled Cincinnatians to "Go Out to the ZOO To-Day and take in the new Baboon, the big bad Elephant 'CHIEF' and the comical half-human chimpanzees 'Mr. and Mrs. Rooney.'"

The zoo knew that Chief had killed his keeper in 1881 when the Robinson Circus passed through Charlotte, North Carolina. They knew that Chief often made his escape from the Robinson stables on Poplar Street, rampaging through the West End. They knew that Chief was known to throw bricks and chunks of coal at his keepers. They knew that Gil Robinson had even

AL BANDLE FIRING THE SHOT THAT KILLED CHIEF.
FROM AN INSTANTANEOUS PHOTOGRAPH TAKEN BY AN ENQUIRER ARTIST.

Al Bandle fires the fatal shot as Old Chief is executed at the Cincinnati Zoo. *From* Cincinnati Enquirer, *December 11, 1890.*

floated the possibility of publicly electrocuting the "notoriously dangerous beast." Instead, in April 1889, Chief was marched from the West End to his new home at the Cincinnati Zoological Gardens.

Chief was a big draw, indeed. But Chief was too much mischief for the zoo to contain. He ripped boards from the floor of his cage and tossed them at zookeepers. He grabbed a dog that happened to run through his quarters and hurled it up against the roof. His antics were endangering the very expensive giraffes next door.

On the evening of Tuesday, December 9, 1890, zoo president Adam E. Burkhardt gave permission to euthanize the big elephant. Adolph Drube, a military marksman, fired eleven shots from a Springfield rifle at point-blank range into Chief's head. By all reports, Chief's temperament actually improved noticeably. He was otherwise unaffected by the gaping wound in his forehead and remained very much alive.

The next day, Wednesday, December 10, 1890, the zoo assembled a small firing squad of local marksmen to finish the job. Al Bandle, Hi Nieman and William Crosby, each armed with a .45-caliber Sharps military rifle, boarded an electric car with zoo superintendent Sol A. Stephan and raced to the elephant house. A crowd estimated at one hundred or more gathered to watch. Stephan decided that it was too difficult to penetrate Chief's cranium, so he painted a white circle behind the elephant's left foreleg, indicating the general location of the heart.

The three riflemen lined up, took aim and fired one volley, to no effect. They fired again and then a third time. A fourth volley sent only two bullets into Chief's body because one of the rifles misfired. At this point, Bandle stepped closer and aimed a shot behind Chief's ear. He fired, and Chief "uttered a terrible screech." It was, the *Cincinnati Enquirer* reported, "his death yell. Those who heard it will never forget it. This shot settled him and the vicious beast fell on his left side, almost rolling onto his back, shaking the wooden building. There was a yell of triumph from the crowd."

The *Commercial Gazette* was disgusted. "It was a bungling piece of work all the way through and reflects no credit upon Supt. Stephan, or the Zoological Garden. The big beast was tortured unnecessarily."

Yet Chief faced further indignities. The crowd of people filling the elephant house had to be shooed off because several tried to carve souvenirs from Chief's ears. A full dissection was undertaken the next day under the knife of Lawrence A. Anderson. Described by the newspapers as "a well-known veterinary," Dr. Anderson was the inspector for the Queen City Mutual Live Stock Insurance Company. Charles Dury, later president of the Cincinnati Society of Natural History, took measurements as he prepared the remains for taxidermy by Ward's Natural Science Establishment. Charles E. Mirguet of Ward's arrived later in the day to begin preservation of the skin and bones.

Everyone wanted a piece of Chief. The *Cincinnati Enquirer* reported, "There was a great rush for steaks and tenderloins and there were thirty-five baskets in Herr Schmidt's cellar belonging to persons who desired to eat elephant meat. W.K. Limbers secured a piece of the tusk, Dr. Anderson an eye, Mr. Spaeth a tenderloin. The tenderloin measured six feet."

Chief's skeletal remains were reassembled and his stuffed skin prepared for display. The Cincinnati Zoological Gardens maintained the exhibit for at least a decade; a 1900 guidebook titled *Studies in Zoology: Cincinnati Zoological Gardens* records that Chief was still at the zoo. Chief was later donated to the University of Cincinnati and later to the Cincinnati Museum Center.

THE SAGA OF PAT MCAVOY, CINCINNATI'S LION SLAYER

Old Chief wasn't the only zoo beast brought low by a marksman. The Cincinnati Zoo was not quite two weeks old on September 30, 1875, when the *Cincinnati Daily Times* printed this rather snarky observation: "It is said that the Zoological Society consists of two persons, Andrew Erkenbrecker and McAvoy. The former furnishes the game for the latter to shoot."

Erkenbrecker, of course, is the man most directly responsible for the creation of the Cincinnati Zoo and Botanical Garden. But who is McAvoy? And what did he shoot?

The answer is carved on a tombstone at New St. Joseph Cemetery in Price Hill. The capstone, badly eroded by acid rain, tells the curious tale of Patrick McAvoy, Cincinnati's "Lion Slayer."

When the defining adventures of his life took place, McAvoy was settled on Ludlow Avenue, raising a family and enjoying an apparently prosperous career as a building contractor and carpenter. He also served as a town marshal in Clifton.

On March 24, 1895, McAvoy was engaged in constructing buildings at the Cincinnati Zoo, which would open that fall. While many of the zoo's buildings were still being assembled, many animals were already on site and housed in temporary quarters. This was the situation involving a testy lioness that was driven by hunger or by instinct to attack a donkey being led past her cage by a young boy. The lioness sprang against the bars of her cage, snapping them like threads, and landed on the donkey's back. The donkey put up quite a fight, inflicting a serious bite on the lion's spine and attacking with its hooves, kicking repeatedly as the carnivore slashed its sides.

A policeman fired at the lion with his seven-shooter without much effect, and night watchman John Nordheim led a small posse armed with a miscellaneous assortment of construction tools and actual weapons, trying to corner the beast. McAvoy joined this ragtag brigade after fetching a shotgun from his tool shed.

Just as it appeared the lioness was hemmed in near the buffalo house, she sprang into the crowd and pinned watchman Nordheim to the ground, sinking her teeth into his thigh. McAvoy marched to within four feet of

BUTCHERS' DAY AND BARBECUE AT THE ZOO.

The annual Butcher's Day at the Cincinnati Zoo saw several prize bullocks dispatched in competition. *From* Cincinnati Post, *August 12, 1897.*

the animal and fired a load of birdshot at close range. The lion let go of Nordheim but leapt on foreman George Haupt and mauled him. Another blast from McAvoy's gun, and the animal was dead.

According to Kevin Grace and Tom White, authors of the 2004 book *Cincinnati Cemeteries*, "It is said that for the rest of his life, he [McAvoy] could walk into any bar in the city and be treated to a drink for his heroism."

McAvoy's reputation as a crack shot and wild-animal slayer was cemented later that fall when a leopard escaped from the zoo and prowled Burnet Woods for a couple of days. It was September 18, 1875, when the first paying customers filed through the zoo's gates. On Sunday of the next weekend, while the new zoological garden entertained twelve thousand visitors, a keeper left the wrong door unlatched and a leopard got loose.

Both Avondale and Clifton—a decade before they were annexed to Cincinnati—had their own constabularies. John Pfeiffer of the Avondale department and Patrick McAvoy, Clifton's marshal, roamed the area looking for the leopard. The leopard announced itself by chasing a gentleman down Clifton Avenue one night.

McAvoy and Pfeiffer cornered the leopard just outside the zoo's fence, no more than a couple hundred feet from where it had escaped. Attempts at capturing it alive proved futile, and once again, Patrick McAvoy was hailed as the marksman who fired the fatal shot. The *Gazette*, deep in a long article, speculates that Constable John Pfeiffer may have inflicted the fatal wound, but "Lion Slayer" McAvoy got the headlines.

The lioness, the donkey and the leopard all met the same fate. They were stuffed and displayed at the zoo for decades.

During the 1890s, a lot of animals were killed at the zoo. As part of the annual Butchers' Day at the zoo, local meat cutters competed to determine who could kill, skin and dress a bull of no less than 1,400 pounds. Although the animals were killed on stage, a curtain was closed at the fatal moment but drawn back to provide a clear view of beheading, skinning and dressing the fresh beef. The deceased bovine contestants were served at a grand barbecue later in the day.

Cincinnati's Celebrated Bridge Jumpers

Some Cincinnati spectacles involved survival rather than death. Bridge jumping, for example. Bridge jumping isn't the career it used to be. Time was, a man could build a solid career by leaping from America's river spans.

Dan Wilcox tragically demonstrated the risks involved when he dove from the Newport Bridge (now known as the Purple People Bridge) on Sunday, June 8, 1890. Before diving into the Ohio River, Wilcox, a longtime river boatman, lowered a rope to determine that the water surface lay 117 feet below the bridge. The *Cincinnati Enquirer* relates the outcome: "The dive was as pretty a one as ever was seen. When a little more than halfway down he

MEREDITH STANLEY'S LEAP.

Meredith Stanley leapt into fame when he jumped from the Suspension Bridge on a bet. *From* Cincinnati Post, *August 11, 1897.*

seemed to lose control of himself. His feet fell faster and faster, and when he struck the water his body was nearly horizontal. The contact was like the sudden crack of a pistol."

Wilcox was pulled from the water and rowed to shore. He managed to stand up, walk to his home on Front Street and sit down in his big rocking chair. There, he gave a few labored gasps and died from fatal internal trauma.

Meredith Stanley had a longer career and greater fame. Stanley had learned the value of publicity when he dramatically rescued two young ladies from the Ohio River in May 1888. Out for an evening cruise, one of the women fell into the stream and almost drowned while the other fainted. The boat drifted uncontrollably downriver. Stanley stripped, dove in, hauled the drowning girl back into the boat and towed the boat back to shore by gripping its mooring chain in his teeth as he swam. The parents of the two rescued damsels chipped in and gave Stanley $100 and a gold medal.

On a five-dollar bet, Stanley made his first bridge jump on Tuesday, July 3, 1888, leaping from Cincinnati's Suspension Bridge into the Ohio River. Unlike the doomed Wilcox, Stanley always leapt feet first. Although instantly famous, Stanley wanted more.

The next spring, Stanley traveled to Lexington for the big one. His Suspension Bridge leap was probably 110 to 120 feet. Just south of Lexington on the Cincinnati Southern Railroad line is the High Bridge, 285 feet above the Kentucky River. Accompanied by witnesses, Stanley made the jump on April 11, 1889. The *Cincinnati Post* reported that a small group of friends from Cincinnati was augmented by a dozen or more curiosity seekers as Stanley perched on the bridge railing:

Stanley bounded far out into the air, contracting himself into a mere ball and drawing his limbs together. Like a shot he fell down, down. It seemed an age to the eager spectators, though but a few seconds to the bold bit of humanity below. High into the air like a suddenly awakened fountain the water rose as with a tremendous splash the human meteor cut the surface.

Although the Kentucky River was only twelve feet deep at the High Bridge, Stanley survived the plunge and took the train back to Cincinnati that evening. Bystanders recalled that he spit up a fair amount of blood, but he claimed no ill effects.

Stanley continued to jump from Cincinnati's bridges for small bets, often chased off by the police. In April 1891, he hurled himself from three local bridges in one day: the Suspension Bridge, the C&O Bridge and the Southern Bridge.

Stanley made a few vaudeville-style appearances, including a stint at the Kohl & Middleton Dime Museum on Vine Street, sharing the bill with the China Sea Devil Fish, Huber the Armless Mouth Artist and the Wooly Woman. The Highland House, up at the top of the Mount Auburn Incline, hired Stanley in 1890 to entertain revelers by leaping from a 115-foot tower into a net. He also got some work diving for the crowds at Chester Park.

After some years as a solo performer, Stanley tried to bring his wife, the former Blanche Mason, into the act. It appears that Meredith and Blanche really did leap off the Suspension Bridge together on New Year's Day 1892. Even though the newspapers reported in some salacious detail about Blanche Stanley's training regimen, in which she stripped naked while her husband poured buckets of ice-cold water over her, no one stepped forward to act as manager. It appears Stanley mostly did vaudeville and sideshows in Cincinnati and was never a regular on the national circuit.

Eventually, the public's taste for bridge jumping waned, and attention diverted to other novelties, like the nickelodeon. Stanley had to go to work for a living and became a steeplejack, painting church spires and smokestacks around the city. That's what killed him at age seventy-four on April 12, 1938, when he fell thirty feet from a smokestack at the old New York Laundry building on Hamer Street.

Compared to the plunges he survived in his heyday, it was nothing to brag about. But for his final plummet, Stanley found only solid pavement below.

CINCINNATI'S VERY OWN VOODOO DOCTOR

King Prince Dawson gained fame just by walking down the street. He said he was a voodoo doctor, and who in Cincinnati was going to prove him wrong? Back in 1888, there were all sorts of spiritualists, Theosophists, agnostics, cultists and philosophers set up in the Queen City—some even

King Prince Dawson, self-proclaimed voodoo doctor, sported the most unusual hairstyle in all of Cincinnati. *From* Cincinnati Post, *July 28, 1906.*

(sort of) authentic. But King Prince Dawson had the voodoo market all to himself.

Although he was a legend in Cincinnati's Black communities, King Prince Dawson first landed in the mainstream media in 1888, when he was charged with performing an abortion. Witnesses saw him exiting a Bucktown tenement in which a young woman was found bleeding next to a fetus of an estimated five months' gestation. Dawson was arrested at his home near Peebles Corner and charged with performing the criminal procedure.

When the voodoo doctor appeared in court, he testified that he did not perform abortions and that whether he did or did not was irrelevant because he was not even in Cincinnati on the day in question. He was, he swore, in Xenia. According to the *Enquirer* of May 8, 1888, this was too much for prosecuting attorney James D. "Dick" Ermston: "Dick Ermston, who is prosecuting the case, said yesterday that he began to believe Dawson was the voodou he has been called, for he seems to have been in Xenia and here at the same time."

Called to testify, Dawson claimed to have no surgical instruments but a knife he used to remove corns, no acquaintance with the woman on whom the procedure had been performed and no knowledge of abortion, and he repeated that he had been in Xenia anyway.

His testimony must have been convincing because King Prince Dawson was acquitted of all charges. The verdict proved disappointing to the courthouse bootblack, known as "Jumbo," who had hoped to claim one of Dawson's mustaches when they were clipped off at the workhouse. He believed he could sell each hair to superstitious folks at ten cents apiece.

Just who was this King Prince Dawson? His name was much in dispute. He went by Dr. K.B. Dawson, Dr. Prince and King Prince in addition to his voodoo name. Some official records list him as Dawson fer Brock or Dawson Brockhaus. Newspapers describe him as visiting Xenia regularly but also traveling south, often returning with substantial sums of money. He boasted of several mistresses and forty children.

Though known to be African American, Dawson also claimed descent from a Cherokee chief and a part-Indian Cherokee princess. He specifically named Hole-in-the-Day (the Elder), a famous chieftain, as a forebear even though

Hole-in-the-Day was Ojibwe, not Cherokee. Dawson also said a Tartar prince and an African princess were united in his family tree or that he was a royal Zulu prince. He carried around documents to prove his genealogy, some written on papyrus. He usually added twenty to thirty years to his age, claiming to be eighty-six or even one hundred when he was in his sixties.

The truth seems to be that his real name was Dawson Brock, and he was born in Kentucky around 1840, perhaps in slavery, and relocated to Xenia before 1870. He was married at least twice and divorced at least once and had two daughters, one of whom may have died young. He served with a Black regiment during the Civil War, possibly as a cook, and operated a grocery store in Xenia before adopting his voodoo persona and relocating to Cincinnati.

It is difficult to imagine anyone mistaking King Prince Dawson for anyone else. He is uniformly described as remarkably tall, over six feet, and his haircut and facial hair must have been unique in Cincinnati. He wore his hair in a broad Mohawk, even though they did not have that word for the style back then. His mustaches—and the papers always referred to them in the plural—hung down nearly a foot on either side of a beard alternately described as either forked or in the "imperial" style.

Dawson usually dressed in a very long overcoat assembled from a zoo full of animal pelts—cat, rabbit, fox, buffalo, seal, muskrat and mink—held together by multicolored stitching and clinking from dozens of medals sewn onto it. His shoes and a shoulder bag he carried displayed ornate beadwork in the Native American style.

The heart of King Prince Dawson's voodoo practice was his herbs and decoctions, and his usual haunts suggest what those preparations were for. He was a regular on George Street and Longworth Street, the heart of Cincinnati's red-light district. He had many clients in Bucktown and Walnut Hills, the major Black neighborhoods at the time. Regular medical doctors avoided all of these neighborhoods, particularly those doctors who prescribed medications promoting birth control or effecting abortions. The evidence suggests that these were the treatments the voodoo doctor carried around in his satchel.

Dawson lived in a shack in a ravine west of Gilbert Avenue near where that street turns into Montgomery Road. When the Cincinnati, Lebanon and Northern Railway ran a route through the area, he was displaced and set up shelters in several neighborhoods. Arrested for stealing chickens in 1906, he spent a few months in the workhouse, where he was completely shaved, to his dismay.

King Prince Dawson had just been released from jail when he was run over by a train while walking the tracks toward Addyston. His left foot was amputated, and doctors thought he might survive. It was not to be. He died a week later.

Dawson's body lay unclaimed for a couple of weeks before his daughter Millie McFarland arrived from Dayton to identify the remains. He may be buried in the United American Cemetery in Columbia Township, but his grave is unmarked.

CINCINNATI'S ZULU QUEEN WAS TOO DIFFERENT FOR WORDS

THE ZULU QUEEN.

The Zulu Queen, known only as "Jim," transfixed and mystified circus crowds and society audiences. *From* Cincinnati Post, *August 8, 1891.*

In 1891, Cincinnati did not know how to respond when someone's behavior marked them as "different." Cincinnati certainly had no vocabulary for the Zulu Queen.

The mystery began with his—yes, his—name, which was Jim. The newspapers did not report a surname for Jim but said he was a popular waiter in "the dining room of a fashionable boardinghouse on Seventh-st." Jim, it seems, waited tables and did "upstairs work" in Cincinnati during the winter. He was, in essence, a butler.

Throughout the summer, Jim performed as the Zulu Queen in old John Robinson's circus. The role was Jim's choice. Jim was recruited into the Robinson troupe by an uncle who performed as the Zulu Chief. Robinson liked the act and asked Jim's uncle to collect a whole Zulu tribe of costumed African Americans. After a season or two, Jim and his uncle had a falling out, and Jim decided to go solo.

It appears that Jim just liked to dance, whether on sawdust or on carpet didn't matter, and that he had another, somewhat classier repertoire he shared with his boardinghouse fans. "Last spring he took dancing lessons for some time before starting out with the circus, and one night he donned his dress suit—mostly pink ribbons and feathers—and gave us a private exhibition in the dining room."

It is obvious that Jim was not only popular but beloved among the habitués of his boardinghouse. The pink ribbons and feathers decorating Jim's private costume sound almost antithetically different from the furs and bones Jim incorporated into his Zulu act. In fact, it sounds a lot like the costumes of the popular "Florodora Girls" of that era. There certainly weren't many male dancers accoutered in pink ribbons and feathers.

The *Post* makes it clear that even Jim's Zulu costume had fashionable aspects, and its description of Jim's Zulu appearance is almost lascivious: "As will be seen by his picture, Jim has the modest sweetness and complacency of demeanor well befitting a Zulu lady of rank. To look at this chubby young queen, with her beautiful arms, her fashionable décolleté bodice and wondrous jewels, who could doubt that she was to the manor born?"

Traveling with the circus, Jim's exotic appearance apparently led to harassment. "Out on the road the boys used to tease him when he got dressed up, and they'd chase him 'round till he'd run in the sideshow tent and hide. He acted in the sideshow."

However, one witness claimed that Jim could dish it out as well as take it: "They used to put the Zulus in a ring and chase 'em on horseback. Jim didn't like to be put in the hippodrome. He was tonier than the rest of the Zulus—he was queen. In the West he used to show his teeth and run at the Indians and go 'um, um' and scare 'em."

Ultimately, the *Post* reporter concluded (having spoken only to acquaintances, never to Jim himself), the whole issue of Jim's sexuality was unresolved. "Two questions remain open: Is Jim a he or a she, and should he be called an African beauty or a Kentucky belle?"

That is a question the *Cincinnati Post* did not endeavor to answer, since no one knew how to discuss gender fluidity in 1891. One wonders what happened to Jim. After this profile, the Zulu Queen never appeared in the newspaper again.

MILES OF MUSTACHE

Miles Osgood didn't even need to walk down the street to cause a sensation. All he had to do was twirl his mustache.

He was known and promoted as the "Possessor of the Most Famous Mustache in America." Miles D. Osgood certainly laid claim to the most amazing facial hair in Cincinnati during the Gay Nineties. He was born in New York and came to Cincinnati as a young man with a mission to clean

MILES D. OSGOOD.

Miles Osgood's monumental mustache appeared almost aerodynamic but mostly served to advertise his chimney-cleaning business. *From* Cincinnati Illustrated Business Directory, *1895.*

chimneys. Not just to clean chimneys, but to clean chimneys better than anyone ever had before. Osgood, who billed himself as the "Chimney Doctor," held several patents on chimney-cleaning technology (but many more patents on fishing tackle). So certain was he of his "mechanical chimney cleaner" process that he offered $100 if a chimney failed to draw.

In addition to chimney cleaning, Osgood owned a moving company, was active in the Knights of Pythias lodge and hawked a custom "Whisker Dye & Tonic." The tonic must have had some efficacy. Osgood died in 1931 at the ripe old age of eighty-one in Jackson, Michigan.

JOHN L. SULLIVAN

Topping anyone famous in Cincinnati back then had to be "Jawn L.," formally known as John L. Sullivan. He was so famous that people who shook his hand became celebrities. "Let me shake the hand of the man who shook the hand of John L. Sullivan" became a Victorian catchphrase.

Sullivan is remembered as the first and the last. He was the first heavyweight champion of gloved boxing and is also recognized as the last heavyweight champion of bare-knuckle boxing. Sullivan was enormously successful, the first American athlete to earn more than $1 million. He augmented his boxing earnings by taking his act onto the vaudeville circuit. It was a stage performance that brought Sullivan and his appetite for demon rum to Cincinnati in 1891. The *Cincinnati Enquirer* of April 23, 1891, tells the tale: "John L. Sullivan made a spectacle of himself during the performance given by his company at the People's Theater last night that was not edifying. Among other things, he said he was drunk, and glad of it."

According to the newspaper, Sullivan was registered at the Gibson House but had made Belle Curry's bordello on Broadway his headquarters. Madam Curry might well have wished the big lug had confined himself to the Gibson, because Sullivan made a mess of her "resort." He kicked over a tray of glasses, beat up an employee named Fannie Frazier and demolished chairs and other furnishings.

John L. Sullivan trounced Dominick McCaffrey at Chester Park in 1885 to gain the heavyweight championship. *From* Cincinnati Post, *August 29, 1885.*

Word of the champ's exploits reached Cincinnati police chief Philip Dietsch, who decided to take matters into his own hands. The chief marched down to the People's Theater and confronted Sullivan.

> *"Sullivan," Chief Dietsch said, "you are a fine specimen of manhood. I wish I was as big and I would tackle you myself."*
>
> *"You are a good sized little man yourself," said Sullivan, "but you will have to excuse me; I have been drinking."*
>
> *The Chief agreed that Sullivan had been imbibing, a good deal.*
>
> *"Well, I am not the worst fellow in the world," Sullivan said, "and I am not as bad as people say I am."*

Chief Dietsch called it a draw, and Sullivan continued to enjoy the freedom of the city. The *Enquirer* opined that Sullivan should appreciate the courtesy he was shown, but one imagines that Chief Dietsch was relieved not to engage in fisticuffs with the heavyweight champion.

HENRY HOLTGREWE: CINCINNATI STRONGMAN

There were witnesses, lots of witnesses, and without their testimony, it is almost impossible to believe Henry Holtgrewe's feats of strength. Tales about the "Cincinnati Strong Man" sound completely inconceivable, even today.

For instance, one day, a friend brought a horse around, hoping to sell it to Holtgrewe. The horse was harnessed to a carriage to demonstrate its speed. Holtgrewe, sitting on the curb with his chair tilted back, grabbed hold of the axle with one hand. As the man cracked his whip, Holtgrewe held the buggy motionless without taking his eyes off the paper. The horse could not move.

Holtgrewe could have made a lot of money doing exhibitions of strength, but he preferred a normal home life. For most of his life, Holtgrewe managed a series of saloons in Cincinnati, where his strength came in handy for dealing with some unsavory customers.

Holtgrewe was running a café on Sixth Street Hill when four rowdies entered his place, bent on trashing it. Henry picked one man up by the ankle and used him for a club, knocking out the other three.

Cincinnati strongman Henry Holtgrewe once lifted the entire Reds baseball team, their manager and coaches, a monkey mascot and assorted barbells. *From* Cincinnati Enquirer, *August 30, 1896.*

Although a formidable athlete and a dangerous enemy, Holtgrewe was known for a heart of solid gold. Once he won $500 in a competition. His competitor told Henry he was flat busted and had six children. Henry gave him all the prize money and sent him back home with presents for the kids.

The most famous weightlifter at the time was a German named Eugen (pronounced *Oy-gen*) Sandow, who had heard about the "Cincinnati Hercules." While touring through Cincinnati, Sandow had his heaviest weights bolted to the stage floor. Holtgrewe showed up and attempted to lift Sandow's barbells. Soon the sound of splintering wood racketed through the theater as Holtgrewe pulled up not only the weights but several floorboards as well.

In 1896, the *Cincinnati Enquirer* hauled Holtgrewe, a load of wood and assorted dumbbells out to the ballpark. Carpenters hammered together a platform of solid hickory, mounted across two sawhorses, loaded with metal weights totaling 1,600 pounds. At a signal, twenty men, plus Jocko, the monkey mascot of the Cincinnati Reds, climbed onboard. Standing beneath the platform, Holtgrewe steadied himself, took a deep breath and then lifted all 4,600 pounds on his back.

Chapter 5

FREAKS, FLESH AND FOOTLIGHTS

Cincinnati once boasted a combination freak show, art gallery, zoo, vaudeville house and natural history collection billed as the "People's Popular Place of Pleasure, and Family Resort" and known as the Dime Museum.

Dime museums were a uniquely American phenomenon and set the stage (as it were) for vaudeville. The typical dime museum boasted multiple floors of curiosities, several small stages and a theater. Objects that today might be seen in a museum of natural history, art museum or historical center would adorn the walls or fill display cases. Sculpture and taxidermy abounded.

Cincinnati's representative of this short-lived phenomenon was Kohl & Middleton's Vine Street Dime Museum and Palace Theater, located on the east side of Vine Street, between Fifth and Sixth. It opened in 1886. As you might guess, admission was one thin dime.

Cincinnati's Dime Museum hosted human oddities such as Jo Jo the Dogfaced Boy, the Wild Man of Afghanistan (apparently a gentle African American man recruited from the riverboats) and Big Winny the Fat Lady, who shared the small stages with magicians and ventriloquists. The Vine Street museum also had a pitiful menagerie of living animals, including bears and exotic birds. In the theater, original comedies such as "The Queen of Lick Run," family orchestras, flying machines, dance recitals, typesetting competitions and even a convention of tattooed people brought in crowds.

Kohl & Middleton's famously booked a band of cowboys to show the Queen City of the West what life was like in the real Wild West. By chance,

Dime museums were an odd conglomeration of freak show, natural history museum, art gallery and vaudeville stage. *From* Darkness and Daylight *by Helen Thomas, 1891.*

Karl Marx's daughter was visiting Cincinnati at the time. The cowboys told her they were not free but exploited workers. The museum also hired bands of Indians, who proved so popular that the Cincinnati Zoo brought in entire tribes to camp on its grounds each summer.

Other headliners included Che Mah the Chinese midget, the Human Giant, the Living Skeleton and the "What-Is-It," who crunched soup bones with his saw-like teeth. It is likely that many Cincinnatians saw their first motion picture at the Dime Museum. A program of Edison Vitascope pictures was featured in 1896.

Neptune's Revenge

A Cincinnati man responsible for the shameful treatment of three beautiful sea creatures learned the hard way that Poseidon protects his own.

Albert Ankeny Stewart was an agent for Aetna Insurance in 1877 when he decided to get into show business by buying a whale—a white whale, a beluga—and having it transported to Cincinnati. Stewart knew nothing, of course, about how to care for the delicate animal, and the results were tragic.

By June 21, 1877, the Cincinnati newspapers were aflutter about Stewart's whale. He had secured it in Labrador and made arrangements to transport it by ship down the St. Lawrence Seaway and by train from New York to Cincinnati. At the Lookout House atop Mount Auburn, a huge tank was built, thirty feet in diameter and ten feet deep, holding 168,000 gallons of salt-treated river water.

Although most newspaper reports suggested that belugas dined on eel in the wild, eel are uncommon in the Ohio River, and a huge supply of minnows from Hamilton, Ohio, was instead laid up for the great beast.

Alas, the whale died en route. A second whale arrived at Mount Auburn but died after just a few days in the tank. A delegation from the Society of Natural History, surgeons W.H. Mussey and A.J. Howe and physician D.S. Young, inspected the corpse and suggested death was the result of starvation; the whale's stomach was empty. The skin and skeleton were sent to a taxidermist for display at the Natural History Museum.

Nothing loath, Stewart procured a third beluga, which arrived about the first of July. This whale remained on display for about a week when a mighty storm blew up. The beluga thrashed about frantically in her tank. At first, observers thought she might be enjoying the storm, but they came to realize she was in distress. Stewart was notified, and he rushed to Mount Auburn in an attempt to save the great beast. "He plunged into the tank," reported the *Enquirer*, "dressed as he was, and commenced to rub the muddy slime off the dying creature. She seemed to understand that he desired to assist her, for she was as tractable under his manipulation as a lamb."

Alas, it was too little, too late, and the third beluga died in her tank. Again, an autopsy showed no food in the belly, which contained many small boulders and the bottom of a glass beer mug. This last whale was about eight feet in length and weighed around six hundred pounds. A shipment of eels, rushed from New York, arrived too late and all dead.

Stewart was a wealthy man when he died thirty-five years later. It was he who convinced Cincinnati's Strobridge Lithographing Company to dive into the circus poster business. Stewart ultimately moved to New York as Strobridge's representative. He and his wife were vacationing in France when he boarded a brand-new ship to return to business in the States.

Poseidon, as it turned out, had other business for him. When an iceberg slashed the hull of the *Titanic*, Stewart sank into Davey Jones' Locker.

A Victorian IMAX

In an age when a significant number of ostensibly educated Americans do not know who won the Civil War, it is unlikely that anyone in the United States today remembers the Battle of Sedan.

In 1885, by contrast, there were very few people in Germanic Cincinnati who had not memorized all the details about the Battle of Sedan, the turning point of the Franco-Prussian War. In one afternoon, September 1, 1870, at this little town in northern France, the Second French Empire fell, the Prussian Empire was born and Europe moved one step closer to World War I. Germans around the world celebrated the anniversary of this victory each year.

German artist Louis Braun, assisted by artists August Lohr and Franz Biberstein, unveiled in 1881 an immense panoramic painting of the battle, more than four hundred feet in length and fifty feet high. Braun was present at the battle and conferred with German military authorities while painting his masterpiece. A company was formed to display the painting in the round at Frankfurt. The massive painting was then displayed in New Orleans through 1884.

On display, Braun's masterpiece was stretched along the walls of a specially designed octagonal building so that the viewer was totally immersed

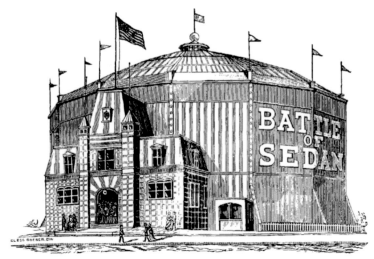

BATTLE OF SEDAN, CORNER SEVENTH AND ELM.

For several years, the most unusual building in Cincinnati was the Panorama, containing a sort of Victorian IMAX experience. *From* Illustrated Business Directory and Picturesque Cincinnati 1887–88.

in the scene. The foreground was built up with dirt and rocks so the painting appeared to emerge beyond an actual landscape. The illusion was enhanced by brilliant electrical arc lighting. The whole effect was something like a Victorian IMAX.

In the spring of 1885, advance agents of the International Panorama Company of Chicago began scouring Cincinnati for a location to bring Braun's extravaganza to the Queen City. By mid-summer, work was underway on one of the oddest buildings ever to grace our town. According to the *Cincinnati Enquirer* of July 19, 1885, "The peculiar and not unattractive building now being erected at the corner of Seventh and Elm streets is shortly to become the home of that great art work the 'Battle of Sedan.' As a realistic picture it has probably never had its equal, and will, without question, be one of the features of our city."

The exhibition opened on August 29, 1885, to rave reviews. The *Cincinnati Gazette* of September 12 was rapturous and saw the opening of the panorama (sometimes referred to as a "cyclorama") as a significant development in economic development and regional tourism: "The great panorama is worthy to be widely known as one of the attractions of the city. If its merit was understood throughout the cities of Ohio, Indiana and Kentucky, and in all the metropolitan and railway districts, excursion trains to see it would be in demand."

Within a week or so, the panorama was attracting "hundreds and hundreds" of visitors. The *Gazette* was prescient in that some visitors came from a distance. By January 1887, reports (no doubt based on press handouts from the International Panorama Company) estimated that "several hundred thousands" of visitors had viewed the *Battle of Sedan*. The exhibit was extended until May of that year, and then it was taken down, packed up and shipped to Toronto for exhibition in that city.

The Panorama building at Seventh and Elm Streets was redecorated and reopened that summer with a new cyclorama painting of the Battle of Gettysburg by French artists Henri and Paul Philippoteaux (father and son). That exhibition opened in October 1887 and was on display during a large Grand Army of the Republic encampment—a reunion of Civil War Union veterans—that same month. Despite their endorsement, *Gettysburg* didn't draw the crowds that the *Battle of Sedan* did. The *Gettysburg* panorama closed at the end of 1888, and the great iron Panorama building was demolished by March 1889, less than four years after its construction.

The vast Louis Braun mural of the *Battle of Sedan* has been lost, as has the Philippoteauxes' rousing rendition of the Battle of Gettysburg.

MAZEPPA'S NAKED RIDE

Adah Isaacs Menken was one of a kind. She was Black. She was Jewish. She regularly shocked society by dressing in male clothing. She gained fame by playing a man on the stage. She was a poet, a painter, an essayist, a sculptor, the highest-paid actress of the age. They called her "The Menken." And she was, for a time, a Cincinnatian.

She was not born here. From an early age, Ada showed a talent for performance, first as a dancer and then as an actor. Her journeys took her from her birthplace in Louisiana to Texas, where she met and married in 1856 an itinerant musician named Alexander Isaac Menken. Alexander was Jewish, and his father was a prosperous merchant in Cincinnati.

Ada converted to Judaism and changed her first name to the more biblical Adah. She took her religious conversion seriously and began submitting essays to the *American Israelite*, published in Cincinnati by Rabbi Isaac Wise. She made her Cincinnati debut in 1858 at the National Theater. It was, the local newspapers noted, "neither a financial nor artistic success."

Adah Menken caused a sensation when she was strapped, nearly nude, to a galloping horse on a Cincinnati stage. *From "Mazeppa Waltzes" sheet music, 1865.*

Fame eluded her until, in Albany, New York, she disrobed as Mazeppa in H.M. Milner's play. This "breeches" role (a woman playing a man's part) was outstanding for two reasons. First, the climactic scene of the doomed Mazeppa lashed to a galloping horse usually involved a stunt double or dummy. Second, Mazeppa was stripped before being lashed to that horse. The Menken did her own stunts and wore a "fleshing," or pink body suit, so she appeared, to audiences of that time, naked.

It worked. Adah Isaacs Menken became both famous and infamous. She became "The Menken." On her return to Cincinnati in 1862, the National Theater sold out almost immediately. The critics raved:

> *The brilliant and peerless Adah—the sensation of the modern stage—last night concluded her first week's engagement at the National. Combining the poesy and daring of one of Byron's loftiest conceptions, she dashes into the "Mazeppa," a character which never would have entered into the imagination of any heroine of the stage to represent, but the heroine of heroines, Adah Isaacs Menken.*

The scandal of her (nearly) disrobed form ended her relationship with the American Israelite. Although she was not really naked while on stage, Adah posed for some topless cartes de visite that still survive.

From Cincinnati, The Menken took her Mazeppa sensation on the road to San Francisco, New York City, London and then Paris. Along the way, she entranced Charles Dickens, had affairs with Alexandre Dumas (Pere) and Algernon Charles Swinburne, married another two men and died in Paris of tuberculosis or peritonitis, or both, in 1868. She was thirty-three years old. Adah Isaacs Menken is buried in Montparnasse Cemetery in Paris. Her tombstone reads only, "Thou Knowest."

LIVING PICTURES

The theaters advertised them as "tableaux vivants." If you were not snooty enough to use French, you called them "living pictures."

Tableaux vivants reproduced famous paintings, usually of the more risqué type, on stage with mostly nude female models who stood perfectly still as an orchestra performed appropriate music. In the case of living pictures, "nude" was a relative term. The models wore flesh-toned body stockings accented by yards of gauze.

Tableaux vivants or "living pictures" employed mostly nude women to impersonate well known erotic paintings. *Cincinnati Enquirer 5 July 1896.*

Cincinnati theaters featured such living picture productions for decades, from at least the 1850s until well into the early 1900s. Although some bluenoses objected, there seems to have been very little interference from the Cincinnati authorities, mostly because these displays were seen as just another method to reproduce fine art.

The fine art in question tended toward the undraped female form, as indicated by the titles of the paintings reproduced as tableaux: *The Fates, The Sirens, Sappho, The Lorelei, Flight, Night, Springtime, Nature's Mirror, Cupid's Counsellor* and so on. The *Enquirer* of April 4, 1865, was typical in its appraisal of living pictures as a valid art form: "At the Palace Varieties there was a big crowd, and the beautiful tableaux of the Keller troupe were applauded to the echo. The exhibition is equally artistic and chaste, and might form a not inapt study for the painter and the sculptor."

There was another reason the authorities gave the living pictures a pass: they were too embarrassed to interfere. When manager John Havlin staged some living pictures at Wood's Theater in 1877, Cincinnati mayor Robert Moore insisted the models add some additional fig leaves. He then, according to the *Cincinnati Star* of April 20, 1877, brought along the police commissioner and the police chief to ensure that Havlin complied. When the moment of truth came, however, the inspectors balked.

> *When, however, Mr. Havlin announced that the statues were ready for the preliminary exhibition, the officials declined to go behind the scenes, but said they would take Mr. Havlin's word for it and permit the show to go on for the night. They took good seats in the audience, and after seeing a few of the pictures declared that the additions to the dress made the exhibition permissible.*

The next year, however, George Ziegler, superintendent of police, told Nat Hyams of Wood's Theater to shut down the living pictures show, according to the *Cincinnati Star* of February 27, 1878: "I was a witness last night of the performance at your theater, and consider the statue tableaux of a character improper for a public exhibition, and under the law an obscene performance."

That particular show might have closed on police orders, but Cincinnati was treated to living pictures shows from all of the major national touring troupes, including Louis Keller's, Matt Morgan's (featuring music conducted by John Philip Sousa), Napoleon Sarony's, Koster & Bial's, Edouard von Kilanyi's and Susie Kirwin's Proctor Theater show.

It appears that young men were not really attracted to the living pictures. Much of the news coverage implies that older men were the primary audience. A note in the *Cincinnati Times* on May 1, 1876, conveys just this suggestion:

> *Matt Morgan's living pictures will show up for all they are worth at the Grand Opera-house tonight. These "living pictures" are able-bodied young women, with a healthy and superabundant physical development and a small show for covering as the pictures exhibited in the saloon windows will testify. People interested in that kind of thing will undoubtedly be on hand by a large majority, and the reflection of the gaslight from the bald heads in the front row will doubtless be quite dazzling.*

Living pictures faded into memory around 1910, replaced by new forms of entertainment, including movies and striptease.

Was Striptease Invented in Cincinnati?

Is Cincinnati the home of striptease? More than one historian of burlesque has suggested exactly that. While there are any number of theories out there on just how striptease originated, a handful of historians have pointed to Cincinnati and, in particular, a publicity-hungry dancer named Millie De Leon and her equally ambitious manager, James Fennessy.

Millie De Leon was what was known around 1900 as a "cooch" dancer. Cooch (or cootch or hootchy-kootchy) was a style of belly dancing popularized at the Chicago World's Fair of 1892–93. There were several women who built profitable stage careers by cooch dancing, the most famous being "Little Egypt."

Millie De Leon was brought to Cincinnati by Fennessy, manager of Hubert Heuck's People's Theater, as part of a resident company of burlesque performers who would entertain between the headline acts. Fennessy was a publicity hound. As manager of Heuck's Opera House and the Lyceum in addition to the People's, Fennessy was mentioned in the papers a lot and quite often for pushing the boundaries of accepted good taste.

When Millie De Leon arrived in Cincinnati, she was almost thirty years old and already known as the "Girl in Blue." At that time, "blue" had a risqué connotation, the same sense that later applied to "blue movies." Fennessy saw potential and recognized Millie's thirst for fame or infamy, whichever arrived first. All Millie needed was a gimmick, and that gimmick was a garter—actually a half dozen garters.

As Millie performed her act, she unclasped a series of garters from her legs and tossed them into the audience. The crowds went wild, especially because Millie conveniently "forgot" to wear her stage tights. The sight of a bare leg was the height of obscenity at the time, and Millie found herself hauled off to the hoosegow in cities across America. Each arrest garnered headlines and bigger ticket sales at the next stop.

James Fennessy realized he had created a phenomenon beyond his control one night in November 1901. A group of seventy-five young men in Over-the-Rhine had organized themselves as a social club named "the Micks." To mark their first anniversary, the Micks planned a midnight dinner with a special entertainment: the Girl in Blue herself.

Millie De Leon agreed to present a very exclusive show for $35—darn close to $1,000 in today's money. The Cincinnati cops showed up, but Millie was hidden away and escaped arrest. Once the police were gone, she was smuggled back into the building. In the basement, Millie "carried out her

Several historians believe that Millie De Leon, the "Girl in Blue," performed the first striptease act in Cincinnati in 1901. *From* New York Daily News, *January 10, 1922.*

part of the programme to the letter. It was long after midnight when the performance was finished, and the statement was made yesterday that everybody went away satisfied 'that he had got his money's worth.'"

Fennessy was apoplectic, insisting that her contract forbade any appearance at stag shows. Millie went on to stardom regardless—mostly on a circuit managed by Fennessy for the Heucks—titillating audiences well into her mid-forties while earning $4,000 a week. She died in 1922, around fifty years of age, in New York City.

In his book *Burleycue: An Underground History of Burlesque Days*, author Bernard Sobel speculates that the "willful removal of one's clothes" on stage began with Millie's Cincinnati garter-tossing. Rachel Shtier, author of *Striptease: The Untold History of the Girlie Show*, notes Millie's pioneering act and specifically credits Fennessy: "Although her name is French (Millie looks suspiciously like Mlle.), she built her early career in Cincinnati and was first tutored by western circuit manager James Fennessey [*sic*]."

She was extolled as "the first real queen of American Burlesque" and "burlesque's first truly national sex symbol" by Robert C. Toll in his book *On with the Show: The First Century of Show Business in America.*

A description of her scandalous dance was recorded in detail by the *Philadelphia North American* in 1914. After removing her outer clothing and tossing several garters, Millie began to "cooch."

> *From knee to neck she was convulsive. Every muscle became eloquent of primitive emotion. Amid groans, cat calls, and howls of approval from the audience, she stopped. Standing suddenly erect, with a deft movement she revealed her nude right leg from knee almost to waist....Streaked and sweaty, her face took on the aspect of epilepsy. She bit her lips, rolled her eyes, pulled fiercely at great handfuls of her black, curly hair. Indescribable noises and loud suggestions mingled in the hot breath of the audience. Men in the orchestra rose with shouts. A woman—one of six present—hissed. Laughter became uproarious. And then, sensing her climax, Millie De Leon gave a little cry that was more of a yelp, and ceased.*

While there is a Burlesque Hall of Fame in (of course) Las Vegas, there does not seem to be a Striptease Hall of Fame. Perhaps this might be an appropriate addition to our Over-the-Rhine neighborhood?

Chapter 6

GRUB PUNISHERS AND MIDNIGHT GOURMANDS

Eating, or rather eating lots and lots, used to be a popular Cincinnati sport. In recent years, Cincinnati has hosted contests for gobbling hot peppers, cupcakes, biscuits and gravy and hot dogs, but none has grabbed the headlines like the champion eaters of yesterday. Back in the 1880s and 1890s, entire neighborhoods showed up to root for their favorite gourmandizers in games of the gullet.

Long ago, Sixth Street ran right up into Mount Adams, where a neighborhood known as Nanny Goat Hill cheered on a very hungry laborer named Pat Maher. One time, Maher followed his friends into Henry Deters's saloon at Ninth and Plum Streets, where the proprietor had laid out the customary free lunch. According to the *Cincinnati Enquirer* of December 15, 1899:

> *The lunch had just been spread, and consisted of roast beef, cold ham, sliced tomatoes, cold slaw, cheese, pickles, bread and several other side dishes. A wager was made that Maher could not clear the table. Maher looked at it a moment and remarked: "Hardly enough for a healthy man." He started, and in a very few minutes the plates were bare.*

In 1889, Maher gained renown for devouring seventy-six eggs, shells and all, at a single sitting.

Down at the Sixth Street Market, the butchers, a hungry bunch, talked about Maher's feat and occasionally claimed they could best him. One such

Joe Ruff had a prodigious appetite, once consuming fifty raw eggs, shells and all, in a single sitting. *From* Cincinnati Post, *September 26, 1913.*

boaster was named Gus Sonnenday. The *Enquirer* of July 7, 1889, noted that Sonnenday had quite a reputation as a "grub punisher." After Sonnenday won several eating contests, his landlord stopped serving him dinner and instead paid his board so he could dine at the St. Nicholas Hotel.

As Sonnenday told this story to the great amusement of the market crowd, a butcher at a nearby stand would have none of it. John Mentzel was his name, and he told Sonnenday that he had eaten ten pounds of ham, five dozen eggs, some fried potatoes, eighteen biscuits and seven cups of coffee for breakfast one day.

Sonnenday called Mentzel a liar. A bet was arranged, with wagers mounting into the thousands of dollars. Someone fired up a grill. Sonnenday challenged Mentzel to repeat the feast, without the biscuits and potatoes—just ten pounds of ham and sixty eggs. In just ten minutes, all of it was devoured and Mentzel declared the new champion.

A peddler named Joe Ruff had a hard time finding a place to live because of his appetite. One landlady threw him out after he ate a dozen of the twenty ears of corn she had cooked for all of her residents. On several occasions, mostly bar bets, Ruff ate fifty raw eggs—shells and all. He regularly ate two or three dozen eggs for dinner.

CINCINNATI'S 1850 CHRISTMAS MEAT PARADE

In all of Cincinnati's bizarre traditions, a parade that flourished at Christmas in the years prior to the Civil War stands out. It was a parade of meat, a vast procession of meat "on the hoof" heading to slaughter, accompanied by marching bands and uniformed soldiers.

In 1850, of course, few households had any means of keeping meat for any period of time, so almost everyone bought meat from the butcher on the day it would be cooked. There was a lot of meat sold on Christmas Day for that evening's dinner.

Cincinnati had six markets in 1850: Lower, Canal, Pearl, Fifth, Sixth and Wade. The Fifth Street Market, which occupied the space now called Fountain Square, was largely devoted to butcher shops. The principal "victualers" were Vanaken and Daniel Wunder, John Butcher (yes, we had a butcher named Butcher), J. & W. Gall and Francis and Richard Beresford. It was these merchants who created the Cincinnati Christmas Meat Parade, according to Charles Cist in his *Sketches and Statistics of Cincinnati in 1851*:

> *A few days prior to the return of this day of festivity, the noble animals which are to grace the stalls on Christmas eve, are paraded through the streets, decorated in fine style, and escorted through the principal streets with bands of music and attendant crowds, especially of the infantry. They are then taken to slaughter-houses, to be seen no more by the public, until cut up and distributed along the stalls of one of our principal markets.*

The meat parade included more than five hundred animals, plus the hired marching bands.

> *Sixty-six bullocks, of which probably three-fourths were raised and fed in Kentucky, and the residue in our own State; one hundred and twenty-five sheep, hung up whole at the edges of the stalls; three hundred and fifty pigs, displayed in rows on platforms; ten of the finest and fattest bears Missouri could produce, and a buffalo calf, weighing five hundred pounds, caught at Santa Fe, constituted the materials for this Christmas pageant.*

The animals were especially decorated for the parade. In addition, Cincinnati's butchers went all out to decorate their market stalls with paintings by the city's best artists:

As Charles Cist reported, in addition to fattened cattle, sheep, pigs and the odd bison, Cincinnati gourmands went in for rarer cuts. Bear meat, especially, was a luxury unknown on the East Coast.

At that time, the quality of meat was gauged by fat content, and the Cincinnati butchers boasted meat so fat that it spoiled before sale because layers of fat insulated the butchered cuts, preventing them from cooling sufficiently, even in subfreezing temperatures.

By noon on Christmas Day, a mountain of meat—primarily beef—had been sold and consumed.

WHEN LUNCH WAS FREE AND TAMALES WERE HOT

Beer goes marvelously well with food, and certain foods just gravitate to beer. Since serious beer consumption tends toward the hours beyond sunset, beer foods become more popular as the night goes on.

Beer has always found itself nestled comfortably next to food. Back in the day, remember, the prominent sign outside your favorite watering hole would have announced something like "A Wienerwurst with Each Drink!" Bar food is a category unto itself, and the offerings today pale in comparison to what you would find at your neighborhood pub in the late 1880s. William C. Smith, in his delightful book *Queen City Yesterdays*, vividly recalls the saloons around his childhood home on Central Avenue in the 1880s:

> *All saloons provided something in the way of free lunch. In most places a simple spread of cheese, sausage, pretzels, pickles, etc., was tendered. Others, operating on a more elaborate scale, served soup and hot meat in addition to the customary layout. A hot dog—which was a good-sized bologna sausage— with two slices of rye bread and plenty of mustard, sold for five cents, with a scuttle of suds at the same price. Ham and cheese sandwiches were five cents each, and the ham was not carved with a safety razor but was thick enough to provide a job for your molars and the rye bread was of the dark variety with a distinct flavor not found in the anemic stuff now on the market. Pig's knuckles and kraut were offered in some saloons—fifteen cents for a man's sized serving and with a reasonable amount of foaming balloon juice to wash it down. This was a treat for the gods—anybody's gods.*

Smith estimated that a single saloon in his neighborhood served more than sixty pounds of meat every day. And that was only for lunch. For dinner, you went home or to a restaurant. Afterward, you returned to the saloon to enjoy the company, argue politics and develop a craving for something tasty. In his 1875 book *Illustrated Cincinnati*, D.J. Kenney describes the itinerant vendors who strolled through Weilert's saloon on Vine Street. Among them was the sausage man:

> *There is another characteristic feature of these saloons and gardens which should not be omitted. The sausage man perambulates them at all hours of the day and evening; but chiefly at half-past nine and eleven in the morning, about six in the afternoon, and throughout the evening, from seven or eight till after midnight. He is as persistent, but not half so insolent, as the London itinerant vender.*

Not to be confused with the sausage man is the Wiener-wurst or Vienna sausage man who came around after the dinner hour: "The Vienna sausage-man is another well-known character 'Over the Rhine.' He is constantly to be met with, and is known by every body. He carries with him a large tin full of sausages, while a small boy by his side bears the bread, the salt, and the pepper."

Of course, pretzels go with beer too. You could find hot pretzels for sale from vendors walking the streets of Cincinnati with heavy baskets hanging from their shoulders. In addition to roasted nuts and popcorn, sandwich vendors strolled the streets past midnight offering a menu that included ham, chicken and cheese selections. In a time when brand names were uncommon, late-night customers looked for individual peddlers known for the quality of their service. You could also find hot baked potatoes from the "Tatoe Man," who pushed his cart, heated by a charcoal stove, through the midnight streets.

The true mainstay of the night owl dining menu was the wienerwurst, not yet called the hot dog. In 1881, the *Enquirer* caught up with a young boy selling wienerwursts so late that the milk wagons were already making their rounds. The reporter described the particulars of the wienerwurst itself, hot and steaming from its tin of boiling water, slapped onto a slab of black or rye bread and slathered with a big dollop of horseradish. The wienerwurst was "nothing more nor less than a sausage, long and slenderly made, not fat and plethoric nor light-colored like the common sausage, but of a reddish, beefy hue. It was piping hot. It was appetizing, and there was a sort of flavor about it that was both strengthening and savory."

A familiar sight in Over-the-Rhine beer halls was the wienerwurst man, followed by his young apprentice with a basket of salt and bread. *From D.J. Kenny's* Illustrated Cincinnati, *1875.*

To a modern-day time traveler visiting this era, one big surprise among the midnight street vendors would have been the hot tamale man. Yes, before Skyline (1949), before White Castle (1921), there was the hot tamale man. It appears that tamales were introduced as street food to Cincinnati around 1880. Patrons gobbled the spicy Mexican delicacies, whether sold from a wheeled wooden cart or from a large can carried by a hot tamale vendor, who was always a man and often blind. Clientele seeking spicy refreshment increased after dark, and there are many reports of citizens complaining about the late-night shouts of the hot tamale men.

Interestingly, although universally referred to as "hot tamale men," these peripatetic vendors sometimes sold no tamales at all. Some sold sausages alongside tamales, and some sold only sausages. When a runaway post office horse demolished Thomas Perry's hot tamale stand, the list of damages revealed a significant lack of tamales. Although known as a "tamale man," Perry sold only wienerwursts, popcorn and peanuts.

Cincinnatians certainly knew what tamales were. Veterans of the Mexican War and the California gold rush brought back reports. Articles about Texan and Californian tamale meals appeared in local newspapers during the 1870s and 1880s.

Cincinnati even had its own short-lived tamale manufacturing plant at 501 West Court Street in the West End. The Tamale Mfg. Co. sold tamales retail at twenty-five cents a dozen. Indications are that the street vendors sold tamales for a nickel apiece—a pretty good markup. John Brock, a hot tamale man, earned enough to buy a fine house on Broadway.

Income at select locations was good enough that hot tamale men fought over the good spots. In 1907, the *Cincinnati Post* reported that seven hot tamale vendors rolled their carts onto the corners of Fifth and Central on a Wednesday night. The competitors began shouting at one another in seven different languages and escalated to fisticuffs before the police arrived and chased them all off.

HOKEY POKEY

Long before Cincinnatians began debating the virtues of Graeter's versus Aglamesis ice cream, we had a yearning for a mysterious confection called hokey-pokey.

You have probably started humming that song, but the "Hokey-Pokey" song you remember wasn't written until the 1940s. When hokey-pokey arrived in Cincinnati in 1885, there was no hokey-pokey dance. The hokey-pokey Cincinnati first tasted was a frozen treat sold from wheeled carts by Italian (and later Greek) street vendors. It's probable that "hokey-pokey" is related to "hocus-pocus" as well as "hoax," because even early on, consumers knew this stuff was not really ice cream. The *Cincinnati Enquirer* of July 13, 1885, described the first introduction of this mysterious treat:

It tasted rich and good, and spoons and saucers were not needed to consume it. It is solidified ice cream, and you can eat a cake as you would a banana or pineapple, holding it in the paper and throwing this away when consumed.
"How long will it keep?"
"In your pocket one hour, while you're eating fifteen minutes."

The *Enquirer* counted only three hokey-pokey vendors in the city in July 1885, each of them pushing a three-wheeled cart with a ten-gallon ice cream freezer mounted atop it, holding perhaps 250 five-cent servings. You paid your nickel and the vendor scooped a slab onto a sheet of newspaper. The new treat proved so popular that three more carts were on order. The hokey-pokey men took to the streets in the afternoon and retired around 9:00 p.m.

By August 1886, there were at least fifteen hokey-pokey vendors patrolling the downtown and West End neighborhoods. Because of the competition, the cost had dropped from five cents a scoop to three cents, or two scoops for a nickel. No one, according to the *Enquirer* of August 1, 1885, knew what hokey-pokey was made from:

The frozen ice-cream is manufactured only by an Italian on West Sixth street. All of the peddlers are required to purchase their hokey-pokey from him. Nobody knows what the stuff is made of. The peddler will tell you that it is "frozen ice-cream," but from the taste it is nothing more than sweetened corn-starch frozen.

Unfortunately for the hokey-pokey men, it was just about this time that governments began looking into the purity of food and dairy products. The investigation was still underway a decade later as reports accumulated that children were experiencing serious illness after eating the chilly street food, whatever it was.

While Cincinnati health inspectors were turning up the heat on hokey-pokey, at least one government official was a big fan. Charles E. James was a justice of the peace in Linwood, which in 1894 was still an independent village outside Cincinnati. Throughout the sweltering

Hokey-pokey had nothing to do with a childhood game in 1885. Itinerant peddlers sold the mysterious frozen confection from three-wheeled carts. *From* Cincinnati Enquirer, *July 13, 1885.*

summer of 1894, Squire James provided two servings of hokey-pokey to every couple that turned to him to officiate at their wedding.

By 1915, the hammer fell on the hokey-pokey peddlers. They could still sell their frozen confection, whatever the ingredients, but they could no longer scoop it out of a common tub onto scraps of paper. The manufacturer was now required to wrap each serving before it left the factory. The fine was fifty dollars and time in the workhouse. (That same day, the city outlawed sales of raw fish from street carts.) The end of hokey-pokey was inevitable.

LEGALLY POISONED CANDY

Hokey-pokey might have been suspicious, but eating Cincinnati candy was like playing Russian roulette. Confectioners openly sold adulterated candy, lethal impurities were widely recognized and the only legal protection was "buyer beware."

The most common adulterants were disgusting but relatively harmless in small quantities. Pulverized gypsum, marketed as terra alba, was popular. With cane sugar wholesaling at more than seventeen cents per pound in 1869, terra alba at two and a half cents afforded a tempting adulterant. Terra alba was so cheap that transport ships filled their hulls with it as ballast and then sold it to candy makers once the freighters docked in Boston. Candy makers openly advertised prices for adulterated versus pure products because there was nothing illegal about adding terra alba to their recipes. For some manufacturers, even terra alba was too pricey; they cut their candies with plaster of Paris.

Other products were far more insidious. Customers have always been attracted to brightly colored candies, and today's manufacturers invest a lot of money in the quest for brilliant and harmless dyes. In the 1800s, manufacturers had no such scruples. The chemicals employed to color candies constituted a hair-raising formulary of toxic pigments. Bright red colors were created with mercury sulfide or lead oxide. Blue often meant some cobalt compound. Yellow was produced by chromate of lead.

Chocolates, also, were ripe for tampering. The *Enquirer* of May 5, 1868, itemized a stomach-turning stew of decidedly non-chocolate additives, indicating that some ingredients corrected the effects of other contaminants to everyday chocolate:

It is amazing our ancestors survived the poisons routinely added to candy before food purity laws were enacted. *From* Harper's Weekly, *December 11, 1858.*

In the preparation of this condiment, cocoa nibs, sugar, fat, flour, sago meal, starch, arrow root, honey and molasses are used; of course, this conglomeration does not retain the desired chocolate color, to obtain which venetian red, umber, and the deadly poisonous metallic salts, cinnabar and red lead are employed; after all this the fatty unctuous of the original chocolate is lost, and must be obtained by mixing in tallow and hog's lard.

For some manufacturers, hog's lard was too pricey. Candy makers used oils extracted from the bodies of hogs, cats, dogs and other animals found dead in the streets.

Even when the manufacturers stuck to normally accepted ingredients, the quality of those ingredients was often less than appetizing. The *Enquirer* of August 1, 1913, reported that sugar, chocolate and coconut valued at $30,000 were condemned at a large local candy factory, having been found "mouldy and wormy" by Sarah Ruhl, food inspector of the city Health Department.

As early as 1882, Cincinnati candy makers banded together in a Confectioners' Union to agree on reasonable standards of purity in the production of candy, but it was only the intervention of city, state and federal inspections after 1920 that allowed a level of confidence that indulging your sweet tooth might not be life-threatening.

Chapter 7

TITANIC TEUTONIC TIPPLERS

C incinnati and beer have been synonymous for more than two hundred years. We love our beer. We have always loved our beer. Estimates from the pre-Prohibition days suggest that your average Cincinnatian consumed more than three times the amount of beer your average American drinks today.

Cincinnatians drank more beer, it is true, but they drank more of everything back then. For example, the cocktail seems to have arrived in Cincinnati about 1855, and it is quite clear from surviving reports that everyone in Cincinnati at that time thought cocktails were the best thing to imbibe before breakfast.

Likewise, we hear much of Griffin Yeatman's Tavern on the banks of the Ohio in old Losantiville. Although Yeatman served locally distilled whiskey and peach brandy, the house specialty was punch. Yeatman's punch bowl—with a capacity above eight gallons—is on display today at the Cincinnati Museum Center.

So, between whiskey, brandy, punch and cocktails for breakfast, a fair amount of intoxicating spirits slaked the formidable thirsts of our pioneer ancestors. When James Dover opened the first brewery in Cincinnati in 1806, after eighteen years of heavy-duty punch and hard liquor, his beer was welcomed in the Queen City like so much sodey-pop.

Daniel Drake, who founded almost everything in town from Spring Grove Cemetery to the University of Cincinnati, was a strong supporter of temperance. He gave many speeches on the evils of alcohol. But listen to this excerpt from his most famous 1828 lecture on intemperance:

> *Strong beer and porter are preferable to ardent spirits; but their daily use leads to corpulence, apoplexy, and sottishness. Table and family beer and porteree (porter diluted with syrup or sugar and water) are far healthier, and never intoxicate. They cannot stimulate a stomach seared with the products of the distillery; but to any other they impart as much excitement as comports with sound health.*

Let us reflect on that significant phrase: "never intoxicate." This was a claim that Cincinnati brewers and their supporters repeatedly advanced throughout the 1800s. Take away our whiskey, you loathsome prohibitionists, they said, but leave us our beer. It "never intoxicates" and it "comports with sound health."

The estimable Charles Cist, the most wonderful historian ever to grace any American city, in his *Sketches and Statistics of Cincinnati in 1859*, describes a vibrant brewing industry with thirty-six local breweries here, producing eight million gallons of suds annually, of which two-thirds was consumed in Cincinnati.

OK, time for some math. That's 8 million gallons of beer, of which two-thirds, or about 5.28 million gallons, were consumed locally at a time when the total population of Cincinnati was 160,000, of which half, or about 80,000, were adults of both sexes, thereby averaging 66 gallons per adult per year. That's a little over a gallon of beer per week per adult. Not so unusual, right? It also happens to be more than three times the annual consumption of beer in the United States in 2018, when the average adult consumed 20 gallons of beer annually, or less than half a gallon of beer per week.

There were at least 1,300 saloons in Cincinnati in 1874. At any rate, there were that many listed in the city directory for that year. The great majority of these saloons were unassuming beer halls, devoted to pouring sudsy lager into schooners or pails. With that much competition, a good saloon needed a gimmick to keep the lager flowing.

It was a rare saloon that didn't house some sort of wild animal or unusual pet, from a talking parrot to a three-legged cat. When someone hauled a giant salamander out of the Ohio River, it was promptly pickled, set out on the bar and advertised to haul drinkers into a Sixth Street dive.

Toward the end of the 1890s, a Cincinnati man hunting in western Colorado captured a full-grown golden eagle. The hunter brought the giant

Good
for
Little
Tots

National Export Beer is good for the children because of the care with which it is brewed by the Moerlein process, after the good old honest German fashion—and of the best materials. It is as pure as can be, healthful and invigorating.

Moerlein's

A. R. CHAMPNEY CO.,
Distributors,   Elyria, Ohio.

With Prohibition looming, Cincinnati brewers tried to reposition beer as a healthy food, even for young children. *From Elyria Reporter, February 21, 1906.*

bird back home and gave it to a friend who ran a saloon out toward the stockyards in Cumminsville. The saloonkeeper let the eagle wander the barroom at will. It accepted raw meat snacks from the customers, poked around in corners and cabinets and abandoned his roost in the cage to take up a perch on the ice chest in back of the bar.

One stormy night in the autumn of 1900, as the saloonkeeper was preparing to shut the place up, a man walked in. The saloonkeeper described him as the "dirtiest, meanest looking and biggest tramp" he ever saw. The man called for a drink, and the saloonkeeper poured him a whiskey. The tramp paid for the drink, to the saloonkeeper's surprise. He was familiar with tramps who drank and only then announced that they had no money.

The tramp took his drink and sat by the stove. It was almost midnight; the weather was cold, and rain poured in sheets outside while thunder boomed. The saloonkeeper had a good fire going and walked over to the stove to stir up the coals. The tramp crept up behind him, knocked him to the floor and began raining blows on the saloonkeeper's head.

With his wits fading, the saloonkeeper cried out, hoping against hope that someone out in the driving thunderstorm might hear him. With a bloodcurdling shriek and a rush of wings, the eagle swooped down from his

TORE PIECES FROM HIS SCALP.

A miscreant miscalculated when he tried to rob a Cumminsville barkeep. The saloon's resident eagle earned his keep. *From* Cincinnati Enquirer, *February 24, 1901.*

perch on the ice chest and buried his talons in the shoulder of the thug, while with his powerful beak he tore strips from the assailant's scalp.

Now it was the tramp's turn to scream for help. He rolled off the saloonkeeper and tried to escape, but the eagle had him in a tight grip and kept beating him with its wings while pulling flesh from his head and shoulders. With a final scream, the tramp fainted on the floor. The eagle released its grip and perched on the back of a chair, where it began to groom its feathers. The saloonkeeper carried the tramp out into the rain and let him lie on the sidewalk halfway down the block. He considered calling the police but decided the tramp had enough punishment.

BLIND TIGERS

Weird monstrosities formed the basis for a popular bootlegging scam called the blind tiger. A "blind tiger" was, in the broadest sense of the term, an illegal saloon. More specifically, a blind tiger was an illegal saloon that used trickery to circumvent the city's liquor laws and its web of graft.

If you didn't have a city license, you couldn't sell drinks. But if you had a city license, you paid for the license and you also paid kickbacks and bribes all year. To avoid the tolls, you opened a miniature dime museum advertising a strange exhibit—a two-headed snake or a blind pig or a blind (stuffed) tiger, for instance—and charged a dime to see it. You then gave away a shot of whiskey to each customer. Since you weren't selling whiskey, you didn't need a license, right?

PRODIGIOUS THIRSTS

And so we come to an infamous article in the old *Cincinnati Commercial* newspaper of August 3, 1879. The headline of the unsigned article was "Big Beer Drinkers: Remarkable Feats of Local Guzzlers." This article was picked up nationally by many other newspapers and appeared in the *New York Times* and *Chicago Tribune* and no doubt contributed to Cincinnati's reputation as a town of Titanic Teutonic Tipplers.

According to the *Commercial*, a city fireman named Peter Farbaugh could drink twelve glasses of beer while the firehouse clock struck noon. Farbaugh, who had retired by the time the article was printed, had been a "reel driver" for the Mohawk Fire Company on McMicken Avenue. The fire company's alarm rang the hours, and the noon bell tolled for about half a minute. Several credible witnesses asserted that Farbaugh had repeatedly gulped twelve glasses of beer of the ordinary size while the fire bell was striking the noon hour. Inspired by Farbaugh's feat, the *Commercial*'s reporter wandered around to some of the Queen City's notable breweries to investigate similar guzzlers.

At the J.G. Sohn & Co. Brewery, he learned about one Dr. L.G. Neffler, who, enjoying the hospitality of the brewery's founder, Johann Sohn, at his home on Mohawk Street, drank an entire eight-gallon keg of beer in two hours.

A horse trader named Henry Dielicht was famous in his neighborhood around Elm and Elder Streets for consuming one hundred glasses of beer—

something like nine gallons—in a single day. Sometimes, it was the thirst for funds rather than beer that inspired these men to quaff vast oceans of malted beverage. Jacob Klein, for example, once drank on a wager of five dollars a full keg of beer in two hours.

Some of Cincinnati's capacity for beer came from the brewery workers who were allowed to drink all they wanted on the job. At Kaufmann's brewery, a worker known as Vantzy commonly downed two hundred glasses each shift. That is a fair amount, even considering that breweries provided fairly small glasses for employee use. Kaufmann's employees usually drank eighteen kegs of beer a day, averaging thirty-five glasses apiece.

Although free beer for employees was common, the amount allowed varied from brewery to brewery. The Gambrinus Stock brewery allowed employees "only" twelve

Although this photo is just a gag shot, there were Cincinnatians who dispatched enormous quantities of beer before Prohibition. *University of Cincinnati Archives.*

to fourteen glasses a day, while Moerlein employees averaged twenty-five glasses a day. At Sohn's brewery, five kegs—forty gallons—of beer were set aside each day for thirty employees. At the Jackson Brewery, employee beer was distributed in carefully calculated amounts.

Now, if the intent of such stories was to prove that beer is not intoxicating, there were some skeptics among Cincinnati's journalists. In May 1882, a Cincinnati jury failed to convict a saloonkeeper named Charles Meyers of violating the Sunday law because that law prohibits the sale of intoxicating beverages on Sunday and the jury could not agree that beer was an intoxicating beverage.

A week later, the *Cincinnati Gazette* conducted an informal survey of prisoners—all women—in police court. The ladies in the dock were unanimous in agreeing that beer was, in fact, intoxicating. According to the *Gazette*, nearly all the women in court said very emphatically that beer drinking had gotten them hauled to the hoosegow.

Now, you may be excused if you think rowdy saloons were a big thing Over-the-Rhine, but they were not. The good Germans north of the canal had beer halls of various sizes, and their neighborhood cafés were generally clean, polite and operated for a family trade.

HILLTOP RESORTS

The best place to drink beer was up on the hills surrounding the city. You got there by riding the inclined plane railroads. We have already heard about the Lookout House and its unfortunate whale in Jackson Park at the top of the Mount Auburn Incline.

A similar resort on Mount Adams was the Highland House, which was located next door to the old Rookwood Pottery. Cincinnati had nothing else quite like the Highland House. The huge edifice accommodated crowds of six thousand to eight thousand every evening. In addition to restaurants and beer gardens, there were bowling alleys, dance halls and a picnic grove. It was the site of political campaigning and six-day walking contests. At the southeastern edge of the complex was the Belvedere, a beer hall with a marvelous view of the Ohio River and the Kentucky shore. So affecting was this riparian panorama that customers dropped their beer mugs while entranced.

The mugs landed in the backyard of one James Carr at 76 Oregon Street. Carr was an engineer at the *Cincinnati Enquirer* printing plant. He and his wife, Margaret, had departed Ireland for the greener haven of the United States in 1834. Their plans did not include beer mugs raining down on their

Highland House brought glamour, festivity and thousands of patrons to the peak of Mount Adams. *From* Frank Leslie's Illustrated Newspaper, *August 7, 1880.*

little slice of the American dream. Carr went to Colonel Enoch T. Carson, Cincinnati's chief of police, to complain that enough mugs had been thrown into his lot within the past year to fill a half barrel.

Bellevue Park atop Clifton Hill was the site of another resort, Bellevue House. It is reported that the owner considered any day in which he did not drain 100 barrels of beer a loss. That's 800 gallons or 6,400 pints.

COCKTAIL SLINGERS

The sophisticated tippler of the 1870s and 1880s had to hunt for something a little more upscale than the standard Cincinnati saloon offered. Luckily, the *Cincinnati Enquirer* published a guide to "Cock-Tail Slingers" on the front page of its issue for June 7, 1874, providing a list of "fashionable drinking resorts."

The better bars in Cincinnati, according to the *Enquirer*, were usually hidden away inside hotels or restaurants and even inside cigar stores. With very few exceptions, the *Enquirer's* list of "interiorly elegant" bars were clustered along Fourth Street between Main and Elm and along Vine Street between Sixth and Seventh. Among the tonier establishments was the Atlantic Garden run by Fred Roos next door to the *Enquirer*, considered to be the "favorite summer evening resort of a mixed multitude."

Jim Callan's Cigar Store on Vine kept a few bottles on hand and was "frequented by politicians of various shades of opinion, who nevertheless coincide in their taste for toothsome corn-juice."

Almost directly across the street from the *Enquirer* building was the Office, run by George Ellis and decorated with paintings and statuary. "It is patronized particularly by the theatrical profession and by men of infinite jest and genius."

Jacob Aug's Club House on Vine hosted "respectable newspapermen, popular politicians, and the most brilliant intellects of our choicest society, snobs being rigidly excluded."

The Cornet, near the corner of Seventh and Vine, was aptly named. The owner was Charles M. Currier, who led one of the city's most popular dance bands. "Only persons of aesthetic taste go there," said the *Enquirer*.

The St. Nicholas Hotel, on the southeast corner of Race and Fourth, featured a bartender named Matt who flourished a diamond breast pin estimated to have cost almost $2,000. (That's more than $43,000 today.) The *Enquirer* guessed that the bar was far more profitable for owner Balthazar Roth than his popular St. Nicholas restaurant.

David R. "Doc" Hickey ran a watering hole known as the Post Office on Vine Street south of Seventh. According to the *Enquirer*, it was the "favorite resort of frisky young bloods, who like billiards, and of domesticated merchants, who like Bourbon straight."

The St. Charles Restaurant on Third Street east of Main "keeps a first-class bar and a first-class woman-killing bar-keeper, with an emerald breast-pin, and languishing eyes."

Out in the West End, opportunities for enjoying, or even surviving, a cocktail were much slimmer. We can rely on the eyewitness testimony of William C. Smith:

> *Cocktails were few in variety and comparatively simple in the West End. Central Avenue saloons, like those on Vine Street north of Seventh, the beginning of the German quarter, then and later were consecrated to the sale of beer. The more sophisticated and elegant saloons in the downtown section and the bars in the hotels, served a greater variety of cocktails and knew how to concoct them. In asking a West End bartender for a mixed drink that required several ingredients and a certain amount of skill in the making, the consumer ran a grave risk. The plain sturdy bartender of our neighborhood was likely to come up with a mixture made by guess and by God, and which, when shot down the red lane to one's interior gave positive evidence that God had a very small part in the process.*

The worst cocktail ever invented might be the so-called Cincinnati Cocktail. There aren't a lot of cocktails named for cities. People usually name the Manhattan first, even though Manhattan is a borough rather than a city, and the same goes for the Brooklyn and Bronx cocktails. The classic mixology guides often include a recipe for Philadelphia Punch, which, while named for a city, is not technically a cocktail.

The same goes for the Cincinnati Cocktail, which appears in bartender guides as early as the 1880s and as late as the 1930s. While it is named for our fair city, it is most certainly not a cocktail in the traditional sense. It is, however, an outrage.

There is a fair amount of leeway in how to mix a Cincinnati Cocktail, but one staple ingredient is beer. The other ingredient is either lemon soda, ginger ale or club soda. The recipe from George J. Kappeler's 1895 *Modern American Drinks* is "a glass half-full of lemon soda; then fill with draught beer."

Jack's Manual, a 1908 guide by J.A. Grohusko, gives a somewhat different recipe, with half a glass of beer, filled up with soda or ginger ale.

The earlier recipe, with lemon soda, approaches what we'd call a shandy or a radler today, while the later versions sound like the odd concoctions Germans drink today.

WHAT DID CARRIE NATION REALLY SAY?

It is among the most treasured quotes in Cincinnati history, right up there with Mark Twain's disputed remark about our town and the end of the world. Almost every book of Cincinnati history features saloon-smasher Carrie Nation's famous quote somewhere, including the revered WPA *Guide to Cincinnati*: "But Carrie did not lift her hatchet arm as she marched up Vine Street; she seemed awed by the formidable array of saloons, beer gardens and concert halls. Asked why she had not broken any windows, she replied: 'I would have dropped from exhaustion before I had gone a block.'"

There it is. One pithy sentence that summed up the utter depravity of the Queen City's saloon culture: "'I would have dropped from exhaustion before I had gone a block." But did she really say it? It sounds like Carrie. It really does. Mrs. Nation was a radical temperance advocate, jailed repeatedly for grabbing a hatchet and smashing saloons throughout legally "dry" Kansas.

As much as that quote sounds like her, it is interesting that none of Cincinnati's newspapers in 1901 reported a quote anything like that from

Carrie Nation scared the mayor's staff witless but smashed not a single pane of glass in the city's saloons during her visit. *From* Cincinnati Enquirer, *March 27, 1901.*

Nation. This was a time when newspapers loved a good quote and loved a good quote that they made up even better.

Carrie Nation's longest visit to Cincinnati occurred toward the end of March 1901. She had been in and out of jail in Topeka for demolition of property. Her lecture tours raised the funds to pay her fines and damage awards. But what did she say?

Although the Kansan firebrand toured the rowdiest dives in the Queen City, she demolished not even the tiniest sherry glass. Nation quietly admitted that she was under $2,000 bond back in Kansas and under strict contract in Cincinnati. Any misbehavior would have sent her back to jail and evaporated her speaking fees.

It is a wonderful myth, but there is no evidence for that quote.

ADOLPH DRACH'S EXPLODING SALOON

Carrie Nation had nothing to do with it, but a Cincinnati saloon caused quite a stir when it exploded in 1896.

Adolph Drach's saloon was one of three in a row located on the east side of Walnut Street, just south of Fifth. Three watering holes in chock-a-block proximity must have generated some competition, and indeed, that appears to have been the case.

If you were to alight from a passing streetcar on Government Square in 1896 and turn down Walnut from Fifth, you would first pass the Esplanade Building on the corner, then Louis Fey's saloon, Drach's and, finally, Theodore Foucar's.

To call Louis Fey's place a "saloon" was somewhat slanderous. True, he sold beer, and lots of it, but Louis Fey thought of himself primarily as a wine merchant.

Theodore Foucar's gimmick was elegance. Foucar's had a large skylight, an immense mirror behind the bar, distinctively stylish glassware and substantial furniture. He was already earning a reputation for the quality of his steaks.

In contrast, Drach's bar, known as the Black Cat, was dowdy and old-fashioned. He inherited the place from his father and knew it had to be spruced up. What could Adolph Drach do to compete? He had invested in carbonation equipment for a fancy soda fountain but needed a real kicker. The answer was electricity.

Both Fey and Foucar apparently lit their barrooms with gas. The light from gas fixtures was warm and inviting, but electricity would brighten

EAST SIDE OF WALNUT STREET, SOUTH FROM FIFTH.

When Adolph Drach's saloon exploded, it demolished half the block on Walnut south of Fifth and shattered windows in nearby buildings. *From Cincinnati Enquirer, May 5, 1896.*

Adolph's saloon, providing a beacon to thirsty tipplers alighting from the Walnut Street cars.

Although electricity had arrived in Cincinnati, distribution was not yet a monopoly, and a citywide power grid was off in the future. There was no single utility stringing wires from a central power plant. A dozen companies sold electrical systems—powered by generators—for the home and business. Adolph Drach contracted with the Triumph Electric Company to install a generator for his saloon.

The electrical plant Triumph Electric assembled in the basement of Drach's saloon employed a gasoline-powered generator, supplied by a sixty-gallon fuel tank that leaked fumes. To turn on the generator, an operator descended into the dark cellar, carrying a candle or lantern. Drach's saloon was basically a large Molotov cocktail.

Adolph Drach's saloon exploded at precisely 7:42:30 p.m. on Monday, May 4, 1896. Eleven people died and a dozen more suffered serious injuries. The explosion completely flattened Drach's and Fey's buildings and punched holes through the walls shared with J.H. Bass's barbershop to the north and Foucar's saloon to the south. All the windows in the Gibson hotel across the street blew out, and two streetcars got knocked off the tracks.

The casualties included Adolph Drach and his four-year-old daughter, who was upstairs in the family apartment. Also dead was Drach's maid, his bartender and a salesman who just happened to be walking by. Drach's wife and son survived with horrible injuries.

The explosion could be plainly heard for several miles beyond the city limits. Rescuers worked through the night under the glare of calcium lights. As they excavated survivors and corpses, remnants of the demolished structures threatened further collapse. Frantic relatives rushed to the morgue, anxiously examining every corpse in fear that a loved one was involved.

HUNGOVER? AVOID THESE CURES

For quite a long time, Cincinnatians had no word for hangover. It is a fairly recent term. Before 1900, "hangover" had nothing to do with booze. For some time, the dreadful after-effects of an alcoholic binge were considered to be an expected outcome of inebriation. Before 1900, "jag" was the word, meaning both the hangover and also the drunken state from which the hangover blossomed.

Nevertheless, from time immemorial, Cincinnatians endeavored to deal with, as Kipling put it, "the cold grey dawn of the morning after." The *Cincinnati Enquirer* of August 11, 1870, pioneered this concept in a front-page article about drunkenness in general and reviewed the traditional hangover cure known as "the hair of the dog." The origin of this remedy can be traced to folklore suggesting that "the hair of the dog is the cure for the bite." In other words, if alcohol brought you to this state, alcohol can relieve your pain.

If more alcohol didn't work, or if the penitent sufferer could not bear the thought of that option, a pharmacopeia of nostrums was available at every Cincinnati pharmacy. The *Enquirer* listed seltzer, citrate of magnesia, valerian, digitalis, tincture of getseminum, morphine, cayenne pepper and even ammonia as palliatives.

The *Cincinnati Post* of December 28, 1915, offered a cure involving a glass of hot water with a teaspoonful of limestone phosphate in it, drunk before breakfast to wash the poisons from your system and cure you of headache while cleansing the entire alimentary canal.

Some inebriates were given to laying handkerchiefs soaked with chloroform over their faces, although the *Enquirer* noted several cases in which that remedy had proved fatal.

Various compounds of gold claimed nearly miraculous power to banish inebriation, hangover or even the taste for spirituous liquors. Various municipalities, notably at Madisonville and Lebanon, Ohio, established gold-cure sanitariums to treat alcoholism. The results were inconsistent, sometimes wildly so.

Chapter 8

RECREATIONAL CHEMISTRY

In a town where alcohol flowed continually, it is not surprising that other intoxicants played relatively minor roles, even though these were the days when everything was legal. Opiates including laudanum and morphine were sold over the counter without need of prescription, as were subsequently banned pharmaceuticals like chloroform, potassium bromide and chloral hydrate. Cannabis, an extract of marijuana, was sold from most pharmacies as well, usually in an alcohol solution. According to the *Cincinnati Times* of April 14, 1873, almost everybody was on something back then:

> *Out of every 1,000 men, 890 use alcoholic stimulants; 950 use tobacco; 260 use opium, hasheesh or morphine; 56 use either arsenic, chloroform or ether; 28 use aphrodisiacs; 230 use chloral hydrate. Out of every 1,000 women, 420 use alcoholic stimulants; 250 use either chloroform, ether or codeine; 20 use morphine; 25 use either arsenic, belladonna, or chloral hydrate; 350 use valerian.*

Cincinnati was fascinated by opium because of its exotic allure. Cincinnati's first real exposure to opium dens came in 1882, when somebody attacked William Todd in a "pipe joint" run by Sam Wing. Todd, no angel himself, had irritated some tough guys in a saloon out on Longworth Street and then retreated to Wing's "rickety old structure" on Walnut Street north of Sixth to smoke. Three men rushed in, slammed a boulder into Todd's head and stabbed him three times. Todd somehow survived and appeared in court to testify against his assailants. According to the *Cincinnati Post* of August 1, 1882, Todd readily confessed to addiction and said he had been ordered to smoke opium by a physician.

A *Cincinnati Post* reporter described on November 29, 1883, his experiences in an opium den located "only two squares from the Grand Hotel on Fourth Street."

> *At first a dreamy sort of languor began slowly to steal over him. His eyes half-closed, and between the partly drawn curtains he could see the dimly lit hall, with the flowers and birds, and hear the tiny "drip-drip" of the fountain. Then the hall changed, and it appeared to him to no longer be a room, but a garden fair in some far-off land.*

THE NEW "DOPE" OUTFIT.

While ignoring opium sales at local pharmacies, Cincinnati police cracked down on dens operated by Chinese immigrants. *From* Cincinnati Post, *July 29, 1898.*

Police and city officials were far from entranced by the opium smokers in the city. Some of their hostility was racial, it is certain, because all the local dens had some connection to Chinese residents. Part of their frustration grew out of the legality of opium at this time. On the same page of a newspaper reporting a crime involving an opium den, readers could find a recipe for home remedies incorporating opium. Mostly, the city fathers just couldn't abide "pipe fiends." Here is the *Cincinnati Enquirer* reporting on August 10, 1884, about opium smokers gathered on Longworth Street: "They stand along the sidewalk, in front of the saloons and cigar shops, with a half-dozen pipes under their felts nearly all the time, and a sickening sight they are, with their sallow complexion and half-drunken appearance."

In addition to the racial aspect, there was also a sexual component to the community's concerns because opium had quite a following among the loose women of the town. The newspapers, missing no opportunity to titillate, made sure to play up this angle, as in this item from the *Cincinnati Enquirer* on November 9, 1883:

> *Pulling aside a curtain made of common calico two females were disclosed lying on the bunks on either side of the little eight by ten "joint." One, the landlady of a Longworth street house of ill-shame, was stretched out on*

Drug use was never far from sexual promiscuity in newspaper exposés of opium use in the city. *From* Cincinnati Enquirer, *November 1, 1891.*

her back with one lower limb across the other. One of her kid shoes was off and lying on the floor. Her dress was opened at the neck, and a yellow faced heathen who was preparing her third pipe occasionally patted her red and seemingly burning cheeks with his dirty hands. The woman, under the effects of two pipes, was in such a condition as to lose what little modesty she ever possessed.

But it was not only the foreigners, the criminal and the poor who "hit the pipe" in Cincinnati. Reporters made regular tours of the opium dens around town—such exposés made great copy and often reported that distinguished businessmen (who remained anonymous, of course) were present and puffing away. On November 1, 1891, the *Enquirer* described a prosperous merchant who rented a cottage on Court Street near Central, where, every evening, he met one of his female employees, not for sex but for the "long draw" of opium.

A 1914 *Post* story describes the raid on an opium den at 133 Shillito Place in which three women and three men were involved. The men escaped through the basement. Two women were arrested, but one woman "connected with a well-known Cincinnati family" was permitted to leave, along with the six-year-old child she had brought along! One of the arrested women also had a child present.

By the 1930s, American names had disappeared from the arrest reports. Federal law now outlawed the drug, and opium seems to have been exclusively consumed by Chinese residents. A 1930 bust found opium dens at 34 West Court Street and 917 Elm. A 1935 raid at 919 Walnut Street netted four smokers and $200 worth of opium, as well as some opium ash used to brew a narcotic (and undoubtedly nasty!) beverage.

No Potheads

Why was marijuana never really popular in old Cincinnati? From the city's founding up into the 1930s, it was entirely legal—but very few people indulged. Despite its ready availability, you will find very few references concerning the use of marijuana for recreational purposes. One rare exception is a brief article in the *Cincinnati Enquirer* of January 9, 1871, in which an anonymous author describes the effects of drinking half an ounce of "hasheesh" solution:

HASHEESH CANDY

An ancestor of today's edibles, Cincinnatians enjoyed cannabis candy during the Civil War. *From Chicago Tribune, April 26, 1864.*

Then commenced a sound of intense sighing that seemed to enter my head, and I felt it revolving faster and faster, until I feared it would break my shoulders. How dim and far away all noises sounded now! The voices in the room were but the faintest whispers. Now and then the seeming motion of my head would stop, and a delicious languor possess me.

Usually, however, druggists prescribed cannabis only for headaches and mild anxiety. Around the time of the Civil War, Cincinnati newspapers advertised "hasheesh candy" with claims that this confection cured all sorts of ailments, from mumps to influenza. An 1864 advertisement promoted more entertaining effects: "It adds beauty as well as years and produces the most mental cheerfulness. It imparts a vigor and strength to the mind and body truly marvelous. Joy and Beauty gladden the Heart."

Despite all the delightful advertising, mentions of this pioneering edible disappear before 1870, replaced by promotions for cannabis syrups and solutions, often touting their effectiveness against consumption (tuberculosis) and asthma.

It appears that smoking marijuana was extremely rare, so unusual that the *Cincinnati Commercial Tribune* of October 5, 1889, found it newsworthy when some Bostonians were discovered puffing away: "Kiff smoking is a new vice which has appeared in Boston. Kiff, or, as it is pronounced, keefe, is a species of hemp which is grown in Morocco, or, rather, it grows there, for it is found wild in all parts of that country."

It appears that some reluctance to indulge in the mystic herb may have been based on a belief that marijuana was poisonous. One doctor, J.B. Mattison, wrote a lengthy article for the *Cincinnati Medical News* in November 1891 advocating for more pharmaceutical uses for cannabis products:

> *Indian hemp is not a poison. This statement is made, just here, because the writer thinks a fear of its toxic power is one reason why this drug is not more largely used. This mistaken idea lessens its value, because it is not pushed to the point of securing a full therapeutic effect. This is a fact....There is not on record any well-attested case of death from* cannabis indica.

Dr. Mattison especially promoted hemp preparations in treatment of insomnia, aches and pains, itching and anxiety.

It is not as though marijuana was unknown in these parts. Hemp was a major cash crop in Kentucky, and tons of hemp fiber were transported to the rope factories of Cincinnati. Marijuana finally caught the attention of Cincinnati during Prohibition. With alcohol illegal, Cincinnati turned to other forms of recreational chemistry. The *Cincinnati Post* of June 17, 1921, reported on a new drink from Iowa called "Happy Wonder":

> *"Happy Wonder" they declared, is made, as is hashish, from Indian hemp, altho instead of chewing or smoking the drug as the Indians do, Iowa farmers are imbibing it in liquid form. One drink of "Happy Wonder," it was alleged by the physicians, makes a farmer utterly scornful of cornfields for days and days.*

By 1931, Cincinnati had declared marijuana illegal. Federal laws soon followed. On October 15, 1931, the *Cincinnati Enquirer* captured the "Reefer Madness" attitude of the time:

> *Vice Mayor John Druffel yesterday succeeded in putting the "kibosh" on "marihuana," "cannabis indica," and "cannabis-sativa," which are technical names for a drug used in making "loco cigarettes." The ordinance, which was passed as an emergency measure, and hence becomes operative immediately, characterizes the weed used in the making of the cigarettes as a "habit-forming drug."*

Even then, Cincinnati laws allowed druggists to keep marijuana in stock to compound medicines until federal laws clamped down on that practice.

CINCINNATI'S EXPECTORATORS
HAVE WOMEN SPITTING MAD

While most men drank in Cincinnati and many enjoyed some sort of drug, by far the most popular stimulant was tobacco. Cincinnati's nicotine addicts rarely employed a pipe, which was seen as either an intellectual affectation or a sign of a country bumpkin. Cigarettes were just catching on toward the later part of the nineteenth century. The primary packages for tobacco consumption were cigars and chewing tobacco. So common was the habit that spittoons, also known as cuspidors, were an essential furnishing for banks, offices, restaurants and well-kept homes.

In 1905, the Cincinnati Woman's Club was fed up with tobacco spitting and lobbied for strict enforcement of the city's anti-spitting ordinance. According to the *Cincinnati Post* of January 13, 1905, the ladies browbeat city health officer Dr. Clark W. Davis into agreeing to do what he could to enforce the law, especially on streetcars. "Mrs. John Dymond suggested that the street car conductors be asked to call attention to the anti-spitting ordinance in the cars and that additional signs of a similar nature be put on street corners, in the corridors of public buildings, in drug stores, cigar stores and other public places."

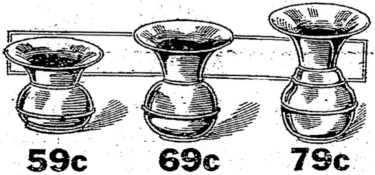

For self-protection, every room in a well-furnished house required strategically placed cuspidors. *From* Cincinnati Post, *December 8, 1913.*

IT HAPPENED RIGHT HERE IN CINCINNATI

This is the Spotter of Spitless Town.

Who spotted a spitter and called him down.

The cuss started cussing, it made the cop sore,

Said he: "Quit your cussing, get a cuss-pidor.

I'll not discuss further, to the jail you'll be led,

Though you ought to go to a ho-spit-al bed."

Cincinnati's efforts to curtail spitting in public often had unintended consequences. *From* Cincinnati Post, *April 4, 1905.*

Dr. Davis protested that streetcar conductors were unwilling to threaten passengers with enforcement. In other cities, conductors who were too vigilant lost their jobs when passengers retaliated by filing complaints. The Woman's Club would hear none of it. The *Cincinnati Post* agreed. In an editorial on February 22, 1905, the progressive *Post* sided with the women:

> *There is public sentiment enough in Cincinnati against indiscriminate spitting to warrant the police in arresting spitters. Of course, the arrests could not be made without some hardship. Spitters are confined to no one class of society. The heavy hand of the law should be as likely to reach the banker as the laborer, and it should, without fear or favor. A few arrests and some modest fines would do much toward awakening spitters to the enormity of their offense, and would also make those who spit and escape the law do some hard thinking.*

As the *Post* implied, the likelihood of a banker being arrested was rather slight, even with actual reports of bankers spitting on streetcars. The first man arrested for violating the ordinance was a molder, along with an electrotyper and a plasterer. There were several reports of bootblack boys being caught and fined.

Eventually, enforcement began to change behavior—though maybe not how the city officials expected. The *Post* reported on May 15, 1905, the complaint of a young lady who said a man had used the back of her dress as a cuspidor to avoid spitting on the sidewalk. In addition, signs in basement windows revealed that spitters now aimed at the windows to avoid hitting the sidewalk.

Chapter 9

NUDITY, NAUGHTINESS AND NEGOTIABLE AFFECTION

Among the Queen City's immoral lures was the Miami and Erie Canal. In 1828, just three years after the canal began flowing, Cincinnati City Council passed an ordinance outlawing bathing in the canal just because of naked men. The ordinance began: "Whereas much lewdness and obscenity daily occur from the public and lascivious manner in which men and boys expose themselves in bathing in the Miami canal in the city of Cincinnati."

By the late 1800s, naked men were still in plain view along the local waterways. But nakedness was not the only crime. Even worse, as a letter writer identified only as "State Avenue" complained to the *Cincinnati Gazette* on June 28, 1878, these flagrantly unclothed males were naked on Sunday. Skinny-dippers, this correspondent claimed, created an offensive impediment to good folks crossing the Mill Creek bridge on their way to church:

> *It is more than enough to have to tolerate the base ball bouncers who congregate all along this pathway to church, about the remote portions of Liberty street, but to have the added attractions of shouting nakedness and juvenile cursing and swearing thrown in, is a little too much for quiet, plain people to bear, and it is to be hoped that an abatement of this Sunday business will follow closely upon the heels of this protest, and the coming Sabbath will be observed with becoming propriety and quietness."*

That "abatement" did not occur because, sixteen years later, there were still folks grumbling about naked men, as reported in the *Cincinnati Post* on June 22, 1894:

> *People in the vicinity of the City Hospital are up in arms. Every day for two weeks past nude boys have been swimming in the canal. Some of them were from 15 to 19 years old. Wednesday a crowd of boys were swimming and standing about the canal bank at the bridge at Twelfth and Plum streets. Crowded street cars pass over the bridge every few minutes.*

Despite complaints from the citizens, the newspapers and the churches, the law proved powerless to halt the march of naked men toward cool pools of water.

LILLIE LANGTRY'S BUBBLY BATH

Far more discreet, yet no less titillating, the most notorious bath in Cincinnati history was drawn one day in 1883.

The bather was Lillie Langtry, known as the "Jersey Lily," an English beauty who, as proof that today's celebrities are not unique, became famous for being famous when she caught the eye of British society. Portraits of her by artists such as Edward Burne-Jones, John Everett Millais, George Frederic Watts, Frank Miles and Edward John Poynter entranced the public. She became the mistress of Charles Chetwynd-Talbot, the Earl of Shrewsbury, and later of Albert Edward, the Prince of Wales (who eventually became King Edward VII of England).

To monetize this fame, Lillie took to the stage. Although by most accounts her acting abilities left much to be desired, she sold out theaters throughout England and then sailed across the Atlantic to capture the hearts (and ticket sales) of America. In February 1883, Lillie Langtry arrived in Cincinnati for an engagement at Robinson's Opera House. As the Jersey Lily's train pulled into the Grand Central Station, Cincinnati was in the midst of a significant flood.

Despite the inconvenience, she found rooms at the Grand Hotel. The famous British beauty asked her maid to draw a bath and discovered that Cincinnati's water in 1883 was pumped directly from the Ohio River, unfiltered. Consequently, the bathtub accumulated several gallons of slop that resembled coffee rather than spring water. After one glance at the murky

The "Jersey Lily," legendary Lillie Langtry, bathed in a tub of Apollinaris water at Cincinnati's Grand Hotel in 1883, undoubtedly lathering with her sponsor's Pears soap. *From* Puck, *March 9, 1887.*

fluid, Lillie refused to subject her beauty to such treatment. She dressed and hurried down to see the manager, who implored Langtry to return to her suite, promising that she should have the clearest of water to bathe in. He then ordered enough sparkling Apollinaris water delivered to her suite to fill her bath. She undoubtedly lathered up with Pears soap, for whom she posed in their advertising.

An enterprising marketer for the Apollinaris water company, on learning of this creative use of his product, had a gold plate engraved to designate room 100 of the Grand Hotel as the "Apollinaris Suite," and that plate hung on the door for the next fifty years. Generations of young men, inspired by visions of Lillie Langtry immersing her voluptuous body into a tub of sparkling water, kept that room occupied for decades.

THE IMMORAL LURES OF CINCINNATI'S PUBLIC LIBRARY

While nude bathing inspired some lewd thoughts, Cincinnati offered a great many occasions of sin ready to entrap young people and drain their moral fortitude. Houses of prostitution and saloons obviously spread their snares, but so did billiard parlors, theaters, circuses and amusement parks. Modern readers may be shocked to learn that Cincinnati spent several decades concerned about the lures of temptation offered by the public library.

On first impression, we might believe that this concern focused on scandalous literature, because Cincinnati still gets in a huff about naughty books. It is true that early librarians were often on the defensive. The *Cincinnati Gazette* of July 30, 1881, in a typical attack, thundered, "There are upon the shelves of the Public Library, intended for general circulation, books of an improper character full of moral poison....The road to ruin begins, in many cases, right at the counter of the Public Library, an institution sustained by taxation and under the control of the Board of Education."

But no, the really big concern about the public library was the ability of men and women to meet in the alcoves to plot sexual escapades of unimaginable depravity.

Seriously.

Blaming the head librarian, Thomas Vickers, for this lascivious behavior, an anonymous correspondent fired off an accusatory letter to the *Cincinnati Enquirer* on October 27, 1874:

> *I am able to prove...that the Library Building is frequented by prostitutes, and that it is used as a place of assignation by young girls. It is a general rendezvous for people who are on the loose. I know a number of young men who boast of the facility which the Library has afforded them in their nefarious business—all under the administration of the austere Vickers.*

Librarian Vickers instituted strict rules to ensure that the sexes were separated as distantly as possible in the library. Men and women, for instance, received the books they requested at separate desks, and women had a dedicated reading room to keep nefarious men away.

There was a serious difficulty in maintaining this moral quarantine—specifically the inability of the library staff to determine at a glance who was innocent and who was depraved. On August 22, 1874, the *Cincinnati Gazette* asserted that the blame did not lie with the designated enforcers:

> *They can distinguish between a man and a woman, but their eyes are not sufficiently educated to tell whether a certain woman is the wife of a certain man. They are obliged to enforce the letter of the law—to make all the men take the one side, and all the women the other. Nearly every day some man becomes incensed at these watchmen, but if the former will only consider a moment, they will see that the latter are only doing their duty.*

Congressman W.C.P. Breckinridge met high school student Madeline Pollard at the public library and then lured her to a brothel on George Street in Cincinnati's red-light district. *From* The Celebrated Case of Col. W.C.P. Breckinridge and Madeline Pollard, *1894.*

All of this worry might have been nothing but local tut-tutting had Cincinnati's public library not featured in one of the most celebrated breach-of-promise lawsuits in the entire nineteenth century. A young Kentucky maiden sued a United States representative from Kentucky named William Campbell Preston Breckinridge. Congressman Breckinridge, according to the plaintiff, Madeline Pollard, stalked her while she was a student at Cincinnati's Wesleyan College for Women. He talked her into accompanying him on a carriage ride, during which he molested her and then arranged an assignation the next day at the Cincinnati Public Library.

According to a book on the case, *The Celebrated Case of Col. W.C.P. Breckinridge and Madeline Pollard,* by Fayette Lexington, published in 1894, Pollard testified that Breckinridge met her at the library but said he could not speak to her there because the rules prohibited conversation. Instead, they took a streetcar to George Street, where a woman admitted them into the parlor of a brothel. Breckinridge maintained Pollard in this house of ill repute for several days before absconding with her to Lexington.

Breckinridge promised to marry Pollard after she bore him two children. She believed him so much that she published engagement announcements in several newspapers. He very publicly married another woman, so Pollard sued and won. In doing so, she dragged the Cincinnati Public Library's reputation through the courts.

CINCINNATI'S LONG-LOST RED-LIGHT DISTRICT

Of course, Congressman Breckinridge would have known about George Street, one of the major streets through Cincinnati's officially designated red-light district. From 1880 until 1917, several blocks in the West End were officially known as the "segregated district," where prostitution was essentially legal.

There were, of course, prostitutes in Cincinnati before 1880. Prostitution was big business in the Queen City almost as long as there have been people in the area. Prostitution and the patronizing of prostitutes was never legal in Cincinnati, but these social vices were not prosecuted outright.

The attitude of the police and courts seems to have been that prostitution was inevitable but should not interfere with polite society or normal business. It appears that arrests were uncommon unless the patrons disturbed the peace. If a brothel got too rowdy, the cops would "pull" it. In such cases, prostitutes were almost invariably charged with loitering and fined between $5 and $25. Madams faced charges of "keeping a disorderly house" or "harboring lewd women" and were fined between $100 and $300. It was common for madams to promise to get out of the business as part of their plea, but it was also common for madams to forget this promise.

Around 1880, Cincinnati followed the lead of New York, Chicago, New Orleans and other cities and created a "segregated district," sometimes called a "segregated vice district," and closed all the brothels located outside it. The district ran from Plum Street west to Mound Street and encompassed three east–west streets: George, Sixth and Longworth. The Cincinnati Convention Center is situated at the southeast corner of this district.

Although regularly referred to as the red-light district, there is not much evidence that houses in the segregated district ever employed red lights to attract customers. It appears that the ladies of the night displayed their names in stained glass to advertise their locations.

Champagne flowed, courtesans danced and the men of Cincinnati winked at laws prohibiting prostitution. *From* Illustrated Police News, *May 2, 1885.*

Within the segregated district, police kept order and kept the brothels open and free of fisticuffs and larceny. A legally defined cesspool of vice of course attracted missionaries eager to save the souls of the fallen, but the city kept the reformers out of the district because the revivalists blocked traffic.

The system collapsed in 1917 as the result of action by the U.S. Army. To promote "maximum efficiency" of its fighting force in World War I, the army promoted the passage of a federal law banning "objectionable" establishments within a five-mile radius of any military training facility. Fort Thomas in northern Kentucky led federal authorities to clamp down on Cincinnati's segregated district.

George Street was considered the heart of Cincinnati's "tenderloin." In 1890, just four blocks of George Street contained forty-six brothels, each supporting an average of five to seven prostitutes. The iconic 1943 WPA-produced *Cincinnati: A Guide to the Queen City and Its Neighbors* still remembered the old days:

> George Street, a short east–west street between W. Seventh and W. Sixth Streets, was the city's most celebrated tenderloin district until the first World War. The three blocks between Mound Street and Central Avenue were lined with brick houses whose red lights proclaimed that Venus presided within. Quiet during the day, George Street sang a litany to venery at night.

George Street was home to such colorful characters as Mollie Chambers, reputed to tip the scales at three hundred pounds, whose brothels often erupted into fisticuffs among the inebriated patrons. Dora Green presided here, too, and the mystery of how she remained unarrested for so long was solved one day when the newspapers reported how she loaned money—lots of money—to police officers on the George Street beat.

The other major thoroughfare in the segregated district was Longworth Street. This infamous avenue once ran from Vine Street westward out past Mound Street almost to the Mill Creek. Longworth's reputation was thoroughly scarlet. At one time, Cincinnati renamed several blocks of Longworth to appease residents who did not want to be associated with that wicked address. Everyone knew, however, that "Carlyle Street" was really sinful Longworth, and Longworth was plenty sinful. A single block of Longworth Street located just south of the Sixth Street Market, and within sight of city hall and St. Peter Cathedral, offered seventeen brothels for libertines to exercise their lust. Today, that block is totally covered by the Convention Center.

DEVOU PARK'S SHADY PAST

The view from Devou Park in Covington is magnificent. Many, perhaps most, people believe the hilltop resort provides the very finest perspective to appreciate Cincinnati. That is certainly the opinion of folks who publish the many postcards featuring panoramas snapped from Devou Park. Very few of the sightseers enjoying the beauties of Devou Park stop to ponder how much their delight was paid for through prostitution and slum tenements.

It didn't start out that way. What we know as Devou Park was originally the family estate of a wealthy milliner named William P. Devou and his wife, Sarah Ogden Devou. The Devou homestead still exists. It is now the older part of the Behringer-Crawford Museum. The Devous' sons, William Jr. and Charles, got fine educations, came home and worked briefly at dad's hat shop. William, in particular, had other plans and began buying property, lots and lots of lots, as it were.

William Devou Jr. owned half the buildings in Cincinnati's red-light district and donated the income to Covington for a park. From Cincinnati Post, *December 27, 1912.*

It was said that William P. Devou Jr. never sold property, only bought more. He was very much a hoarder. He made a fortune renting his many properties by the day, the week or the month. Rents ran three to seven dollars a month for a room, more for a house. His rent receipts were printed on two sides. One side had the receipt form, and the other was an eviction notice if the tenant skipped a rent payment.

The majority of William Jr.'s rentals lay in Cincinnati's red-light district. He owned around 120 buildings there. Many of these were elegant and sumptuously furnished brothels, but that appearance was due to the madams who ran the houses, not because of the cheapskate landlord, who rarely spent a penny on repairs. Devou was constantly in court paying fines for allowing his impoverished tenants to live in grossly deteriorating tenements.

When Devou's parents died, the sons donated the property to Covington for use as a park. When William Devou Jr. died in 1937, his real estate was held in trust for several years, with a bank collecting rents from the old brothel properties. Alfred Segal, columnist for the *Cincinnati Post*, observed on December 10, 1937, the irony involved in the disposition of Devou's slum holdings: "It seems rather amusing for tenement houses in Cincinnati's West End to keep on producing rents for the upkeep of trees and flowers in Covington."

BEWARE THE MASHER

The historical record attests that far too many men are unable to behave appropriately around women. They had a word in 1905 for pesky, would-be Lotharios who spoke to women on the sidewalks or in the streetcars. They were called "mashers."

A masher was any man who addressed a woman to whom he had not been formally introduced. The only women who tolerated such outrages were common streetwalkers. Consequently, every respectable woman approached by a strange man, no matter how politely or discreetly, considered herself insulted.

What sorts of utterances counted as "brazen attentions" or "insulting remarks"? Few newspapers gave the sordid details, but one story quoted a masher asking a woman outside a theater, "Waiting for me, darling?"

No masher in his right mind would have dared shout at or catcall a woman walking past him on the street. Such brazen offenses would have been suicide. Any man within earshot would have rallied to defend the woman's honor by attacking the catcaller. Such was the impetus that inspired Joseph Mayer, Covington fire chief, to soundly thrash a masher on Madison Avenue one summer evening. An unidentified young lady was

It always made news when a woman retaliated on a masher, any man rude enough to address her on the street. *From* Cincinnati Enquirer, *October 6, 1889.*

looking at the Covington store windows, according to the *Cincinnati Post* of July 13, 1897, when she was approached by an impudent young man, who insisted on speaking to her. She walked up to Chief Mayer, explained the situation, thanked the chief after he knocked the masher into the street and continued on her way.

Women who smashed mashers made national headlines. A masher unwisely sauntered up to a group of young ladies about to embark on a steamboat cruise from the Public Landing, according to the *Cincinnati Post* on June 25, 1895:

> *Approaching them, he made an insulting remark, and posed for the answer, which he was convinced his stunning appearance would command. But he had reckoned without his host, for a moment later blows were raining down on his worthless carcass from a cane skillfully wielded by the plucky little lady, and with the assistance of her companions that lovely pongee coat and vest were in shreds and a dude's hat missing.*

Fists, canes, umbrellas all figure into reports of women defending themselves, and many a masher learned painfully that hat pins can do more than secure millinery to the feminine hairdo.

Not all "mashing" was committed in public. The term *masher* came to refer to any man who attempted to seduce almost any woman. Set aside for particular opprobrium were married men who presented themselves as unattached bachelors. The Ohio General Assembly passed a specific law outlawing these cads in 1894. It was known as "The Married Masher Act." Cincinnati prosecuted a man named George Partlow under this law when he seduced a young Newport woman and "maintained improper relations" with her for a week while leading her to believe he was unmarried.

Self-Abuse and "Youthful Errors"

All this pent-up erotic energy often found relief through private stimulation, and Cincinnati was obsessed with autoerotic pleasure during the 1800s. It was nearly impossible to read any Cincinnati newspaper from the 1850s well into the 1890s without running into advertisements about masturbation or, as they usually called it back then, "self-abuse" or "youthful errors." Several Cincinnati doctors specializing in "private diseases" offered to cure the unfortunate victims of this practice.

GRAY'S SPECIFIC MEDICINE.

The Great ENGLISH REMEDY.

TRADE MARK. **TRADE MARK.**

An unfailing cure for Seminal Weakness, Spermatorrhea, Impotency, and all Diseases that follow as a sequence of Self-Abuse; as Loss of Memory, Universal Lassitude, Pain in the Back, Dimness of Vision, Premature Old Age, and

Before Taking **After Taking.**

many other Diseases that lead to Insanity or Consumption and a Premature Grave.

☞ Full particulars in our pamphlet, which we desire to send free by mail to every one. ☞ The Specific Medicine is sold by all druggists at $1.00 per package, or six packages for $5, or will be sent free by mail on receipt of the money, by addressing

THE GRAY MEDICINE CO.,
No. 10 Mechanics' Block, DETROIT MICH.

Sold in Cincinnati by JOHN KEESHAN, F. L. EATON. ERNST WILFERT, and all Druggists.

JOHN D. PARK & SONS, Wholesale Agents.

The Cincinnati newspapers regularly published advertisements for doctors or patent medicines dedicated to curing the effects of self-abuse. *From* Cincinnati Star, *December 26, 1878.*

Drs. J.D. Kennedy and J.D. Kergan, in an advertisement in the *Cincinnati Post* on December 20, 1898, called on their dissipated readers to "rouse yourself and be a man." They made clear that this moral failure was widespread:

> *The result of ignorance and folly: over-exertion of both mind and body induced by lust and exposure, are continually wrecking thousands of promising young men. Some fall before they enter the active duties of life, while others, undermined by the results of self-abuse or lust, after a few*

years are forced to drag out a weary, fruitless and melancholy existence. The victims are found in all stations of life—the farm, the office, the pulpit, the trades, the professions—all supply them.

Kennedy & Kergan practiced at the tony address of 122 West Fourth Street, very close to the offices of Cincinnati's top bankers, lawyers and merchants. Dr. A.B. Spinney lumped self-abuse among a horrific roster of "private diseases" that he treated in his office at 518 Race Street. According to his ad in the *Cincinnati Post* on November 30, 1897, Dr. Spinney claimed thirty-five years of successful experience: "We positively cure sexual and nervous debility, emissions, drains of power, wasted organs, self-abuse, impotency, varicocele, hydrocele, syphilis, gonorrhea, gleet, stricture, pimples, and all blood and skin, bladder and kidney diseases, quickly and permanently, without detention from business."

It has likely been some time since a Cincinnati doctor diagnosed gleet (a watery discharge) or stricture (narrow urinary tract), but varicocele (distended scrotal veins) and hydrocele (fluid build-up in the scrotum) are still medical terms in common use.

Several of the men who advertised cures for self-abuse hastened to assure readers that they were authentic doctors. Dr. Clark Jacques, for example, used the very first sentence in his advertisement in the *Cincinnati Enquirer* on April 22, 1871, to proclaim that visitors to his office at 130 West Sixth Street could examine his diploma on full display.

Cincinnati's medical community did not ignore the possibility that women also engaged in self-pleasure. The effects, as described in the Cincinnati medical journal *The Lancet* in 1867, were much more benign than those men suffered:

> *Dr. [Robert] Greenhalgh considered that the frequency and evil effects of self-abuse in the female had been greatly exaggerated. He did not believe that it led to idiocy and epilepsy as had been assumed; that girls suffering from these affections were occasionally addicted to such a habit he did not deny. He did not believe that the clitoris or nymphae had anything to do with the habit, but that it must be rather referred to a peculiar mental condition requiring moral control.*

Although it is obvious that the pursuit of private pleasure did not abate, changes in medical practice and advertising standards resulted in all such advertising disappearing from the Cincinnati newspapers after about 1900.

Chapter 10

BOSS COX'S FIEFDOM

Cincinnati, during much of the period covered by this book, was controlled by a political machine. At the controls was a man named George Barnsdale Cox, still known today by his nickname, "Boss Cox." We can dedicate this book to old Boss Cox because he made possible most of what you have been reading about.

Political machines are run on money, but legal money only goes so far. A good political machine needs bribes and graft and good old-fashioned corruption, and Boss Cox had all that in spades. Good corruption needs vice, and Boss Cox made sure that Cincinnati was a wide-open town. "Open" meant free-flowing booze at all hours and all day Sunday. It meant convenient and almost honest gambling. It meant lots of women of negotiable affection. And it required lots of shady street contracts.

To keep the votes rolling in for his chosen politicians, Cox dispensed county funds where loyalty could be bought. The Cox Machine ignored the city's parks because, as they joked, the squirrels didn't vote. Cox bled the schools because teachers didn't vote and, as one of Cox's lieutenants was quoted, "most of them are women, anyway." Street improvements, on the other hand, were golden. A good street paving job bought the contractor, some subcontractors, suppliers and workmen, and every one of them chipped in a kickback to get the job. According to an exposé on Boss Cox in *Collier's Magazine* on January 6, 1912, "Paving was a favorite form of outlay. The successive machine administrations paved and repaved. Instead of patching

Boss Cox and his minions, Rud Hynicka, Garry Herrmann and Mike Mullen, get the boot in a wishful but premature cartoon. *From* Cincinnati Post, *November 5, 1906.*

the worn spots, these guardians of the public good would tear up the whole job and relay it. Every cobblestone, every flag, every curb in Cincinnati, is a monument to Boss Cox."

Cox's ambitions were such that he needed a constant influx of new money, and this insatiable greed led to Cincinnati declaring war on Westwood.

THE WESTWOOD WAR

In the early 1890s, Boss Cox and his machine looked up to the hills surrounding Cincinnati's crowded basin and set their sights particularly on five adjacent villages: Avondale, Clifton, Linwood, Riverside and Westwood.

In planning to annex these five villages, the downtown powers saw at least four things. They saw the opportunity for additional tax revenue without raising tax rates. They saw the potential for even more tax revenues as more residents moved to the hills. They saw numbers. The Cincinnati basin by 1890 was heavily settled with no room for population growth. By adding land, lots of land, lots of open land, Cincinnati had the opportunity to report a significant increase in population by the next census.

Most importantly, Cox and his boys saw Republicans. As chairman of the Hamilton County Republican Committee, Cox knew that these satellite villages leaned strongly Republican. He also knew that they leaned strongly independent. If Cox asked the five villages to vote on the issue, he knew that they would vote to stay independent. Most of the voters in the five villages saw a big neighboring metropolis wallowing in debt, ruled by a shady, even criminal, regime. They wanted no part of that mess.

So, Cox changed the rules. He marched up to Columbus and had the state legislature pass the Lillard Law. (The law is named for Robert W. Lillard of Cincinnati, who introduced the law while serving in the Ohio General Assembly. The Cox Machine later rewarded him with a sinecure as superintendent of city hall.) This law mandated, in questions of annexation, that the votes of the villages to be annexed must be counted along with the votes of the city to which they would be annexed. In other words, Cincinnati's 50,000 voters would be asked to vote on annexation along with the 2,200 voters in the five hilltop villages. The five targeted villages learned an important lesson about Boss Cox: You can't win. You can't break even. And you can't quit the game.

Which brings us to the 1897 election of Gustav "Gus" Tafel. Cox was correct when he predicted the hilltops would vote Republican. He had not counted on the hilltops voting progressive Republican and supporting the Democratic Citizenship ticket headed by Tafel. All of the new hilltop wards, including Westwood, went for Tafel. Newly elected Mayor Tafel knew he held these voters by the thinnest of threads. He had to produce for them, and they wanted city services—lights, streetcars, waste collection, water and especially police.

When Westwood began to complain about the patrons of the saloons out at the end of the streetcar line, Mayor Gus Tafel paid close attention. The Westwood War of 1899 erupted over the unruly honky-tonks out on the far west side.

The big new suburb of Westwood had only been a Cincinnati neighborhood for three years, but it was already a big western headache for Cincinnati police chief Phillip P. Deitsch. When Cincinnati gobbled up the hilltop suburbs, it annexed eleven square miles of additional territory but did nothing to increase the size of the already overworked Cincinnati Police Department. Delegations of Westwood citizens went downtown to demand a permanent police station in Westwood or at least a patrol wagon. Mayor Tafel told Police Chief Deitsch that he wanted law and order enforced in Cincinnati's newly acquired "Wild West."

The many newspaper articles about the rowdy Westwood saloons bothered Alonzo Hildreth, one of Westwood's former mayors. He objected to the slurs against his neighborhood and complained that the real troublemakers were in Cheviot.

COLONEL DEITSCH: "WHEN I LOOK THROUGH TAFEL'S SPECS WESTWOOD IS NOT SO FAR AWAY AFTER ALL."

Cincinnati police chief Phillip P. Deitsch agrees that Westwood is not so far distant when he looks through Mayor Gustav Tafel's glasses. *From* Cincinnati Post, *July 14, 1899.*

Well, yes and no. Five saloons located right on the streetcar line caused most of the complaints. Two were in Westwood, and three were in Cheviot. The worst offenders were Charles Orr's Cheviot saloon at Glenmore and Harrison and Ed Connor's Five Mile House at the corner of Harrison and Montana in Westwood.

The first volley in the Westwood War was fired at midnight on January 1, 1899. The very first arrest in Cincinnati that year was Westwood's own

George Dater, hauled in for discharging firearms within the city limits. As the year went on, the city's streetcar conductors led the charge as they complained about rowdy passengers returning from Westwood. According to the *Cincinnati Post*, "Conductors on the Westwood cars have appealed to Chief Deitsch to put a stop to the scenes of revelry and disorderly practices on street cars returning from Westwood. Rough characters have been returning to the city in a hilarious condition and giving the street car men no end of trouble."

In July, a domestic dispute erupted within a streetcar on the Westwood line. Two Cincinnati officers, Charles Bevington and Charles Blanchard, watched an argument begin at Charlie Orr's place in Cheviot. They had no jurisdiction there and so followed the battling trio onto the inbound streetcar, where it became apparent that the woman cuddling with waterworks employee Charles Baumgartner was not his wife and the woman with the bloody lip wailing on the illicit pair was his lawful spouse. The *Cincinnati Post* gave a description in the best tradition of Gay Nineties journalism: "There was another disgraceful row at Westwood Monday night. A woman, bleeding at the mouth from a blow administered by a man, was seen struggling and wrestling with another female on the last car from Westwood. The car was crowded."

The *Cincinnati Enquirer* found another streetcar fight "exciting." It appears that James Finn, a downtown barkeep, had a few drinks in Cheviot and objected to the conductor hitting a buggy halfway down the Harrison hill, so he punched him. This proved to be a mistake because the conductor beat the living daylights out of Finn and then continued the ride into town with his assailant lying bloodied in the aisle.

Although Mayor Tafel lit a fire under Chief Deitsch, the Cincinnati Police response had all the appearance of a "Keystone Kops" comedy. In May, the city sent three officers out to patrol the streetcars, but the conductors complained no officers had shown up. On investigation, Lieutenant Samuel Corbin found the officers wandering almost a mile away from their assigned posts.

In July, a bouncer at Edward Connor's "resort" at the corner of Montana and Harrison had to restrain a Cincinnati patrolman who was misbehaving on duty. As reported to the *Cincinnati Post*:

> *A regular policeman of the Cincinnati force was there Sunday night, danced with young girls, flourished his revolver, and wanted to start a "rough house." He was so drunk…that it was necessary to lead him out of the*

place, take away his revolver and slungshot [blackjack club] *and lay him out on the grass to sleep off the effects of his debauch.*

Cincinnati Police sent a troop of patrolmen out to Westwood on Sunday, July 16, and they kept the peace, but they eventually returned to headquarters. The *Post* reported, "Westwood 'cut loose' Sunday after the officers from the city had disappeared. Scalp wounds, black eyes, and disfigured countenances were numerous. For fully an hour a street brawl raged."

Finally, Chief Deitsch sent an officer out with a warrant. The Westwood War had begun. Under a headline of "War Begins on Rag-Time Resorts Near Westwood," the *Cincinnati Post* exalted, "The first shot was fired Tuesday by the police against Westwood when Detective John Calnan swore out a warrant for the arrest of Charles Orr, proprietor of one of the rag-time resorts at the end of the Westwood car line, alleging that he keeps a disorderly house."

The *Cincinnati Post* had a blast reporting on the comic attempts to rein in the Westwood disturbances, running a huge front-page cartoon of outrageous chaos in Westwood with a suggestion that the police chief could only see the trouble by borrowing the mayor's eyeglasses. The news coverage included a map illustrating the Westwood "stronghold" as a big mug of beer. It is labeled "Ground map of the Westwood field operations, showing the fortifications of the enemy and the treacherous nature of the approaches."

Although the news coverage hammered Westwood, and although Ed Connor's Five Mile House had some unruly clients, the big offender at the very end of the Westwood car line was Charles Orr in Cheviot. The *Enquirer* detailed the charges against Orr: "The police claim that it is a rendezvous for young girls who drink more than they ought to. There has been a number of fights there, and only yesterday a delegation of citizens from Westwood appeared before the Board of Police Commissioners and protested against Orr's place and others where disorderly conduct is permitted."

Despite the fact that his saloon and his residence were outside the city limits, Orr appeared in Cincinnati Police Court. As expected, the question of jurisdiction arose immediately. Interestingly, the question was not only about Cincinnati's jurisdiction over a Cheviot or Green Township saloon but also about the Police Court's jurisdiction over Westwood under any circumstances. Apparently, there were details of the annexation agreement yet to be finalized. When the case did come to trial, the case against Orr evaporated. Prosecuting Attorney William H. Lueders completely folded. Police Court judge Edward Schwab was beside himself:

Why don't the citizens of [Cheviot] *incorporate and legislate against such places if they are so disagreeable? They are asking our protection and for what? As the Prosecutor says, it does not seem justifiable to put the city and its taxpayers to the expense of the trial when the citizens of* [Cheviot] *are not citizens of Cincinnati, and are not contributing to that expense.*

The judge ended up leaving the charges on open docket, which prohibited Orr from suing the Cincinnati Police and leaving the possibility of reinstating the charges. Orr closed his dance floor by filling it with tables to allow more drinking, so at least that awful ragtime music was banished.

Cheviot took Judge Schwab's scolding to heart. About sixty Cheviot residents gathered in Singer Hall on July 12, 1899, determined to incorporate. An election was held on June 8, 1901, and Cheviot voted to incorporate.

Westwood finally got its police patrol wagon. Remember Mayor Tafel? He lived in Fairview and decided that the Patrol 8 Wagon at the Fairview precinct was underused and could be loaned to Westwood a couple of days each week.

It wasn't enough. In 1900, Westwood voted along with all the other hilltop neighborhoods in sending Boss Cox's handpicked candidate, Julius Fleischmann (who happened to be a major whiskey distiller), to the mayor's office. Westwood's saloons continued to make the news from time to time, but the war was over.

COMFORT STATION GRAFT

They were toilets, public toilets, but to mollify Victorian sensibilities, Cincinnati called them "comfort stations." The Fountain Square comfort stations were created in controversy. Much of this controversy erupted within the Cox Machine.

Since this was the era of machine politics, every city employee—even the attendants employed at the new Fountain Square comfort stations— held jobs controlled by political patronage. The question was, which city office controlled the patronage (and the accompanying kickbacks)? Was it the parks department? Or was Fountain Square a market, in which case the Board of Public Service pulled the strings?

For curious legal reasons, because it replaced the old Fifth Street Market, Fountain Square is, technically, a market, so the Board of Public Service prevailed, awarding attendant jobs to its friends and taking a small slice of their pay in gratitude.

Street Names Honor Boss Cox's Minions

Loyalty to Boss Cox could mean permanent recognition via a Cincinnati street sign. On Friday, September 4, 1908, the *Cincinnati Enquirer* carried a substantial legal advertisement, comprising four columns of dense type announcing Ordinance 731 as ordained by Cincinnati City Council: "To change the names of certain streets, avenues, courts, terraces, places and alleys of the City of Cincinnati as designated therein."

What followed was a list of hundreds of Cincinnati streets that, partially or completely, would receive new names by order of the city administration. The *Enquirer*, which had cozied up to the political machine, printed the ordinance without comment. The *Cincinnati Post*, a constant burr under the saddle of the Cox Machine (and therefore the recipient of no city advertising), smelled a rat. In that day's edition, the *Post* identified the rodent:

> *Cincinnati having no Hall of Fame, Cox's Council has honored his faithful servants by naming streets after them. For, after erasing names of 50 old streets, Council has substituted names of its own members, and what streets were left were named for members of the Mayor's office, the Service Board, the Police Department, the City Solicitor's office, the City Engineer's office, and even favored friends who don't hold city jobs, but who do control certain and diverse votes.*

Buried in that long list of renamed streets were more than fifty for which the new name honored someone in the city administration, and everyone in the city administration owed their jobs to Boss Cox. Heading the list was Mayor Leopold Markbreit, whose name now graced the former Williams Avenue. The mayor pleaded humble ignorance: "I tell you it's impossible to tell when, or where, or how lightning will strike, likewise honors. A few years ago I never expected to have even a cat named after me. I'll have to find out where Markbreit-av. is and see that it is kept clean."

Vice Mayor John Galvin got a street in Lower Price Hill, where the former Belmont Avenue became Galvin Avenue. But it wasn't just the top administrators who got their names assigned to streets. The mayor's secretary got a street in Avondale. A street in Fairmount was selected to recognize Louise Amthauer, stenographer to city council (and the only woman on the list). Kuhfers Alley, between Findlay and Charlotte Streets in Brighton, still memorializes Police Detective Conrad Kuhfers. Hopkins Avenue in Avondale was renamed to honor Thirteenth Ward councilman J.H. Asmann Jr.

All you have to do is to name a street after a Gangster. Then property holders will sell dirt cheap.

When Boss Cox's gang decided to name streets after themselves, the anti-Cox newspapers claimed the move created memorials to gangsters. *From* Cincinnati Post, *September 9, 1908.*

Cox, to be sure, kept his fingerprints away from this little gambit. The outrage fell on city council. In particular, the ringleader was revealed to be Edwin O. Bathgate, representing the Eighteenth Ward. Bathgate sat on council's Streets and Parks Committee and submitted the names in that capacity. A loyal Cox foot soldier, Bathgate had recently been indicted for buying votes.

Many of these streets still bear the names of Boss Cox's minions.

THE NAUGHTY YELLOW BANK FISHING CLUB

Perhaps the best insight into life in the Boss Cox era is demonstrated by an annual orgy, and the wildest parties of Cincinnati's Gay Nineties were organized by…a fishing club?

Indeed. The Yellow Bank Fishing Club really did fish. Most of the members appear to have been policemen, firemen or merchants. The longtime president of the club was William Wiechering, a city building inspector. News stories implied that members also represented the city's commercial elite, with their "names over the doors of six-story establishments" or "nearly all of the city officials and City Hall attaches."

"WALTZ ME AGAIN."

Hot stockings and short dresses brought out the gawkers whenever the Yellow Bank Fishing Club threw a soiree. *From* Cincinnati Enquirer, *January 27, 1898.*

The club met monthly in the West End and owned a fishing camp on the Whitewater River, near Brookville, Indiana. To help raise funds for the camp, the club launched a series of balls in 1893. Invitations to the 1894 ball promised that it would be "hotter than Tabasco sauce" and apparently made good on that promise. The early parties were staged at the West End Turner Hall on Freeman Avenue. The 1897 ball, according to the *Cincinnati Post* of January 17, 1897, was particularly successful:

Many a toiler on the way to the factory or shop Thursday morning stopped at the entrance of the West End Turner Hall to watch a gay rounder as he bundled his companion into a cab and drove off beside her. They had been to the Yellow Bank Fishing Club Ball and stayed to the finish. The ball was a financial success and at midnight every room in the big Turner Building was crowded to suffocation.

The attractions included generous bartenders, hot dancing and lascivious ladies. Even though several patrons were ejected every year for disruptive conduct, the ball, occupying three floors of the Turner Hall, was Cincinnati's hottest ticket.

In the barroom below, stages were rigged up with tables and the scenes that followed rivaled the Midway in its palmiest hour. There was dancing wild and weird. The fun raged fast and furious, and at one time when the band in one of the drinking-rooms struck up the famous "couchee-couchee" every table became an impromptu stage with a half-dozen contestants.

By 1900, the ball had become something of an institution but maintained its image as a risqué debauch. Crowds of people who wouldn't dare go inside gathered in the frigid night outside the Turner Hall on Yellow Bank evenings to appraise the costumes of the young ladies as they arrived. They would holler, "There's a warm one!" when they caught sight of a particularly well-turned ankle or a set of provocative hosiery.

Others did not share the appreciation. Cincinnati's Humane Society (which looked out for the welfare of children and juveniles) charged the Yellow Bank Fishing Club with admitting girls younger than sixteen into the ball. Police raided the 1900 ball, closing down the bars and charging the proprietor of the Turner Hall with serving liquor past midnight.

The Turners had enough and evicted the Yellow Banks. Undaunted, the fishing club moved its 1901 ball to Workmen's Hall in Over-the-Rhine. The next day, headlines blared "Wild Orgy!" and the breathless report suggested that the Yellow Bank ball had maintained its saucy reputation at the new location. The *Cincinnati Post* reported on February 15, 1901:

Cincinnati's all-night balls reached their limit Thursday night and Friday morning at the hilarious revel of the Yellow Bank Fishing Club at Workmen's Hall. Old timers who have attended rag-time balls for years back, declare they had never seen anything like it. The orgy grew faster and more furious as the morning hours sped on.

Three floors of the West End Turner Hall were packed with revelers at the Yellow Bank Fishing Club ball. *From* Cincinnati Enquirer, *January 23, 1900.*

The paper reported prodigious drinking, women dancing on tables, daring costumes (particularly a number of young ladies clad in military garb) and rowdy groups of university students.

The Yellow Bank Fishing Club popped up in the newspapers for a decade after 1901, but the coverage was benign. There were reports of baseball games, fishing camps and pranks played by members against one another. The club made so much money from the balls that a moderate dues increase in 1902 covered the costs of their summer camp, with no need to involve the cops, the ministers, the Humane Society or the mayor.

BY 1920, THE CITY I have just described was all gone. Prohibition closed the saloons. Military regulations during World War I shut down the red-light district. Organized crime took over the gambling and moved it to Kentucky. The movies killed vaudeville and the racy theaters.

All we have left are the memories.

SELECTED BIBLIOGRAPHY

Aaron, Daniel. *Cincinnati: Queen City of the West 1819–1838*. Columbus: Ohio State University Press, 1992.

Cist, Charles. *Sketches and Statistics of Cincinnati in 1859*. Cincinnati, 1859.

Clarke, Robert. *The Pre-Historic Remains Which Were Found on the Site of the City of Cincinnati, Ohio: With a Vindication of the "Cincinnati Tablet."* Cincinnati, 1876.

Cromwell, Helen Worley, with Robert Dougherty. *Dirty Helen: An Autobiography*. Los Angeles: Sherbourne Press, 1966.

Dabney, Wendell P. *Cincinnati's Colored Citizens*. Cincinnati: Dabney Publishing, 1926.

De Beck, William L. ("An Old Citizen"). *Murder Will Out*. Cincinnati, 1867.

Drake, Daniel. *Natural and Statistical View, or a Picture of Cincinnati and the Miami Country*. Cincinnati: Looker and Wallace, 1815.

Ford, Henry A., and Kate B. Ford. *History of Cincinnati, Ohio*. Cleveland: L.A. Williams & Co., 1881.

Goss, Charles Frederic. *Cincinnati, the Queen City, 1788–1912*. 4 vols. Chicago: S.J. Clarke Publishing, 1912.

Grace, Kevin. *Cincinnati's Literary Heritage*. Charleston, SC: The History Press, 2021.

Grace, Kevin, and Tom White. *Cincinnati Cemeteries: The Queen City Underground*. Charleston, SC: Arcadia Publishing, 2004.

Greve, Charles Theodore. *Centennial History of Cincinnati and Representative Citizens*. 2 vols. Chicago: Biographical Publishing Company, 1904.

Haller, John S., Jr. *A Profile in Alternative Medicine*. Kent, OH: Kent State University Press, 1999.

Hall, Joseph John. *The Great American Rosetta Stone*. Tampa, FL, 1949.

Harlow, Alvin F. *The Serene Cincinnatians*. New York: E.P. Dutton and Company, 1950.

Jones, A.E. *Extracts from the History of Cincinnati*. Cincinnati: Cohen & Co., 1888.

Juettner, Otto. *Daniel Drake and His Followers*. Cincinnati: Harvey Publishing, 1909.

King, Moses. *King's Pocket-Book of Cincinnati*. N.p., 1879.

Leonard, John W. *The Centennial Review of Cincinnati*. Cincinnati: J.M. Elstner, 1888.

Lloyd, John Uri. *Etidorhpa or the End of Earth*. Cincinnati, 1895.

Ludwig, Charles. *Playmates of the Towpath*. Cincinnati, 1929.

Miller, Francis W. *Cincinnati Beginnings*. Cincinnati: Peter G. Thompson, 1880.

Miller, Zane M. *Boss Cox's Cincinnati: Urban Politics in the Progressive Era*. Columbus: Ohio State University Press, 1968.

Moore, Gina Ruffin. *Black America Series: Cincinnati*. Charleston, SC: Arcadia Publishing, 2007.

Nelson, S.B. *History of Cincinnati and Hamilton County Ohio*. Cincinnati, S.B. Nelson & Co., 1894.

Roe, G.M., ed. *Our Police*. Cincinnati, 1890.

Shotwell, John B. *A History of the Schools of Cincinnati*. Cincinnati: School Life Company, 1902.

Smith, William C. *Queen City Yesterdays*. Crawfordsville, IN: R.E. Banta, 1959.

Starr, S.F. *The Archaeology of Hamilton County, Ohio*. Cincinnati: Cincinnati Museum of Natural History, 1960.

Suess, Jeff. *Lost Cincinnati*. Charleston, SC: The History Press, 2015.

Symmes, Americus. *The Symmes Theory of Concentric Spheres*. Louisville, KY: Bradley & Gilbert, 1878.

Taylor, Nikki. *Frontiers of Freedom: Cincinnati's Black Community, 1802–1868*. Athens: Ohio University Press, 2005.

Tolzmann, Don Heinrich. *Over-the-Rhine Tour Guide*. Milford, OH: Little Miami Publishing Co., 2011.

Trollope, Frances. *Domestic Manners of the Americans*. London: Whitaker, Treacher, & Co., 1832.

Woellert, Dann. *Cincinnati Candy: A Sweet History*. Charleston, SC: The History Press, 2017.

————. *Historic Restaurants of Cincinnati*. Charleston, SC: The History Press, 2015.

Writers' Program of the Works Progress Administration of Ohio. *Cincinnati: A Guide to the Queen City and Its Neighbors*. Cincinnati: Weisen-Hart Press, 1943.

Various editions of *Cincinnati Commercial Tribune*, *Cincinnati Enquirer*, *Cincinnati Gazette*, *Cincinnati Post*, *Cincinnati Press*, *Cincinnati Star*, *Cincinnati Times*, *Frank Leslie's Illustrated Newspaper*, *Harper's Weekly*, *Puck*, *Judge*, the *Illustrated Police News*.

ABOUT THE AUTHOR

Greg Hand is the proprietor of the *Cincinnati Curiosities* blog. He began writing for the *Western Hills Press* while still in high school and, after graduating from the University of Cincinnati, worked for several years as a reporter and eventually editor for the *Press* newspapers. He returned to the University of Cincinnati, where he headed the public relations office. During his time at UC, Hand coauthored three books about the university with Kevin Grace. Since his retirement from the university, Hand contributes history content regularly to *Cincinnati Magazine* and the WCPO-TV *Cincy Lifestyles* show. With Molly Wellmann and Kent Meloy, Hand presents entertaining history chats in bars and saloons through a program called "Stand-Up History."

Visit us at
www.historypress.com